THE ROAD TO THE SPRING

THE ROAD TO THE SPRING

Collected Poems of Mary Austin

Edited By James Perrin Warren

Syracuse University Press

First Edition 2014

14 15 16 17 18 19   6 5 4 3 2 1

∞ The paper used in this publication meets the minimum requirements of the American National Standard for Information Sciences—Permanence of Paper for Printed Library Materials, ANSI Z39.48-1992.

For a listing of books published and distributed by Syracuse University Press, visit www.SyracuseUniversityPress.syr.edu.

ISBN: 978-0-8156-3345-7 (cloth)   978-0-8156-5275-5 (e-book)

Library of Congress Cataloging-in-Publication Data

Austin, Mary, 1868–1934.
[Poems. Selections]
The road to the spring : collected poems of Mary Austin / edited by James Perrin Warren. — First edition.
pages cm
Includes bibliographical references and index.
ISBN 978-0-8156-3345-7 (cloth : alk. paper) — ISBN 978-0-8156-5275-5 (ebook)
I. Warren, James Perrin, editor of compilation. II. Title.
PS3501.U8A6 2014
811'.52—dc23   2014015202

Manufactured in the United States of America

Contents

Acknowledgments

For permission to reprint poems from *The American Rhythm* (1923, 1930) and *The Children Sing in the Far West* (1928), I gratefully acknowledge Houghton Mifflin Harcourt Publishing Company. The University of Utah Press kindly gave permission to quote extensively from *Mary Austin's Southwest*, edited by Chelsea Blackbird and Barney Nelson. Editors at magazines and journals whom I contacted for permission were helpful in suggesting that they no longer held copyright on Austin's poems.

This edition of Mary Austin's poems would not have been possible without the support of the Huntington Library in San Marino, California. I was fortunate to receive two short-term fellowships from the Huntington to conduct research on the project: a one-month stay in the summer of 2002 as the Kenneth E. and Dorothy V. Hill Fellow, and a three-month stay in the summer of 2008 as an Andrew Mellon Fellow. I am grateful to Barney Nelson for supporting my applications for fellowships at the Huntington. During those four months of research, the staff members working in the Ahmanson Reading Room were always professional, courteous, and even friendly. Especially good to me were Sue Hodson, Curator of Literary Manuscripts, and Dan Lewis, Chief Curator of Manuscripts. In the early mornings before the reading room opened, Dan graciously introduced me to the birds and other wildlife in the Huntington Gardens.

My home institution, Washington and Lee University, provided generous financial support for summer research and writing. The John M. Glenn Grant program and its successor, the H. F. Lenfest Grant program, have given me steady funding for thirty summers, and four of those summers funded work on *The Road to the Spring.* The Lenfest fund for publication subvention provided funds to obtain permission to republish from Houghton Mifflin Harcourt Publishing Company. In addition, I thank my colleagues in the Department of English, especially Suzanne Keen, for their belief in the project. Suzanne's deep response to my public reading of Austin's poems on campus meant more to me than I can easily say.

Special thanks go to my former student Eric Gehman, who created the index. Editorial support from the staff at Syracuse University Press, especially Jennika Baines, was superb. For expertise and sharp eyes in copyediting the manuscript, my thanks to Jessica LeTourneur.

Friends from the Association for the Study of Literature and Environment (ASLE) have given me abiding encouragement and long-term support. Among many others, John Tallmadge and Michael Branch deserve special mention for their nearly stone-blind belief in my work.

Finally, I thank my wife, Julianne Lutz Warren, an inspiration in her conscientious intellectual passion. She, my heart's friend!

Abbreviations

AR 1923	*The American Rhythm* (1923)
AR 1930	*The American Rhythm* (1930)
AU [folder number]	The Mary Hunter Austin Papers, Huntington Library
LJE	*Land of Journeys' Ending* (1924; rpt. 2003)
MASW	*Mary Austin's Southwest* (2005)

A Note on the Texts

This edition is the first collection of Mary Austin's poems to be printed. The Mary Hunter Austin Papers at the Huntington Library in San Marino, California, are the principal collection of Austin's work and the most important source for the poems in this book. By combing through the boxes of the Austin Papers, I found numerous copies of poems printed in magazines and periodicals, as well as the manuscript poems in the final section of the edition. In all cases I refer to the manuscripts and offprints of the poems by the folder number of the Austin Papers. Hence an important notebook of early manuscript poems appears in AU 381.

In editing the poems for publication, I have been most concerned to present accessible, readable texts for students and general readers. When Austin's spelling is antiquated or idiosyncratic, I have let it stand. When it is an obvious misspelling or mispunctuation, however, I have silently corrected the error. The annotations are kept to a minimum. I gloss terms that a modern reader may find obscure or difficult, especially those that pertain to Native American cultures of the Southwest and California. I use an asterisk when necessary to mark a stanza break.

THE ROAD TO THE SPRING

A Modern *Chisera*

Born in 1868, Mary Austin lived through a period of significant cultural transitions, beginning in a recently reunited, post-Civil War United States and ending in a global industrial power on the eve of World War Two. In literary terms, she began in the era of Harriet Beecher Stowe and Emily Dickinson and ended with the emergence of Willa Cather, H. D., and Marianne Moore. From the 1890s to her death in 1934, Austin was steadily productive, publishing dozens of poems, short stories, novels, plays, and essays. Her writing was widely known and often highly praised by some of the best critics of the day, including Mark Van Doren and Carl Van Doren. She had deep roots in regional literature, promoting the prose and poetry of writers like Vachel Lindsay, Carl Sandburg, and Robinson Jeffers. She also helped to advance Imagism, the first important modernist movement in twentieth-century poetry, and she could claim Alice Corbin Henderson, Amy Lowell, and Harriet Monroe as friends and colleagues.

Austin identified most closely with the desert country of the Paiute and Shoshone Indians in Owens Valley, California, where she lived as a young woman in the final decade of the nineteenth century. At the turn of the twentieth century, she was often part of the literary gatherings of the editor and writer Charles Lummis in Los Angeles, and in the first decade of the twentieth century she lived in the bohemian writers' colony of Carmel, on the coast near Monterey, making a name for herself alongside Jack London, George Sterling, Upton Sinclair, Robinson Jeffers, and Lincoln Steffens. Just when modernism was appearing in the art and literature of Paris and London,

Austin was a well-known figure in the literary world of New York City, living there from 1912 to 1924. In the last decade of her life, she found a home in Santa Fe, New Mexico, doing important work in preserving and promoting the arts among the Pueblo Indians and Hispanic settlers. Both an outsider and an insider for the nearly forty years of her writing career, Austin was a recognized voice in the rapidly changing American literary scene.

Modern readers know Austin best for a handful of essays and stories, most published in the early years of the twentieth century. The vivid prose of *The Land of Little Rain* (1903) remains Austin's most original work. Published by Houghton Mifflin when Austin was thirty-five, the book still appeals strongly to readers and is often listed as an essential book in environmental literature. Readers of *The Land of Little Rain* readily catch the voice of a maverick, an outlier, a feminist, and a rebel. The book has kept Austin's ideas alive in discussions of environmental literature, feminist writing, Native American studies, and regionalism. But Austin began her writing career as a poet, and she wrote poems throughout her career. Moreover, Austin's poetry shows the evolving voice of an environmentalist, an ecofeminist, and an experimenter in free verse.

In addition to the tough-minded renegade, Austin creates a powerful new figure in her poems—the *Chisera*, or Medicine Woman. The Chisera is a female shaman, at once a visionary prophet, social critic, and healer. The Chisera first appears in Austin's verse drama *The Arrow Maker* (1911) as a conflicted, tension-ridden character. Caught between her love for the ambitious arrow maker and her duty to her community, the Chisera finds her true path by abandoning the vulnerabilities of human emotion and embracing the strengths of contemplative solitude. Austin wrote two different endings to the play. In the production version, the Chisera supplants her lover and becomes the visionary leader of her people, taking them into righteous war. In Austin's preferred original version, the Chisera dies at the hand of her faithless lover as she announces the victorious path to her people.

For Austin, the role of the visionary Chisera is literary and cultural. The writer functions to show her people the road to truth—a road that will take the people back to the sources of their goodness and power as a community of believers. This is what Austin means when she calls for us to travel "the road to the spring . . . to the source of man's medium, rather than to his emotions; a road which every people must take from time to time if it would not see its own most intimate expression smothered in staleness, ossified by tradition."[1] The writer shows her people where the road leads into the future; indeed, the road to the past leads to the future. Because Austin found the figure of the Chisera in the cultures of Native American tribes in the Southwest, she saw the role of the visionary as bound into the mythological, religious beliefs and cultural practices of the American Southwest. To combat the alienation and disaffection of modernity, the Chisera would provide new ways of putting beliefs into practice. Even though Austin did not fully embody the role in her own career as a writer, she clearly saw that the Chisera would be a visionary artist and mythmaker. In several phases of her career, moreover, Austin connected that visionary role with the function of poetry in modern life. For example, in the preface to *The Arrow Maker* she defines the Chisera as "simply the Genius, one of those singular and powerful characters whom we are still, with all our learning, unable to account for without falling back on the primitive conception of gift as arising from direct communication with the gods" (*Arrow Maker* xi–xii). Austin directly connects the figure to "the present social awakening to the waste, the enormous and stupid waste of the gifts of women" (xii). The specific role of the woman writer is to combat the waste of women's gifts by an oblivious community.

1. "The Road to the Spring," *Nation* 123 (1926), 360–61. The essay is reprinted in *Mary Austin's Southwest: An Anthology of Her Literary Criticism*, ed. Chelsea Blackbird and Barney Nelson (Salt Lake City: University of Utah Press, 2005), 205–8. Further references to this anthology appear in parentheses, cited as *MASW.*

If the Chisera plays a crucial role in awakening and reforming the tribe, she is also at the mercy of the tribe. The Genius is singular and powerful, but she is not immune to the effects of social circumstance. Austin's sense of the tensions between the singular Genius and the manipulative "society at large" recalls the Romantic conception of the poet, as Percy Bysshe Shelley formulated it in the final sentence of "A Defence of Poetry": "Poets are the unacknowledged legislators of the world." The tension between legislation and lack of acknowledgment is palpable, despite Shelley's grand optimism. Likewise, Austin sees the double bind of the writer in a world of social awakening, but she never relinquishes her belief in the Chisera. That belief is most acute and tenacious in relation to Austin's career as a woman writer, and her poems reveal the writer in a particularly compressed and dramatic form. That is especially true in the poems that stem from Austin's lifelong passion for Native American rituals, but it is also apparent in other poems about place, people, and politics.

An Ancient Track to the High Places

Although Austin was not the first writer to claim a relationship between Native American art and modern American poetry, Michael Castro rightly describes her as "one of the most active and influential of the early twentieth-century writers who redefined the meaning of the Indian for American culture."[2] For example, the February 1917 issue of *Poetry* featured "aboriginal poetry" in free-verse forms, including two poems by Austin, and in the same issue Carl Sandburg's note on Frances Densmore's *Chippewa Music* connected Native American songs to Imagism and Vorticism (Castro 17–18). Austin's influence broadened with the publication of an anthology, *The Path on the Rainbow*, in 1918. Edited by George W. Cronyn,

2. *Interpreting the Indian: Twentieth-Century Poets and the Native American* (Albuquerque: University of New Mexico Press, 1983), 5. Castro devotes most of the first chapter to Austin (5–45).

the book included translations of Native American songs by ethnologists like Alice Fletcher, James Mooney, Washington Matthews, and Franz Boas, along with one "translation" by Austin herself. Perhaps more important, it published "interpretations" by five poets, including seven poems by Austin. At least as radical as the collection of songs and poems, however, was Austin's introduction, in which she claimed the central influence of "Amerindian art" (her preferred term) on modern American poetry.

The authenticity of Native American poetry relies on its intimacy with place, and Austin uses that authenticity to ground a relationship between Amerindian art and twentieth-century American poetry. Austin's bold three-part argument is encapsulated in a paragraph from her introduction to *The Path on the Rainbow*:

> The poetic faculty is, of all man's modes, the most responsive to natural environment, the most sensitive and the truest record of his reactions to its skyey influences, its floods, forests, morning colors. It is the first to register the rise of his spirits to the stimulus of new national ideals. If this were not so there would be no such thing as nationality in art, and it is only by establishing some continuity with the earliest instances of such reaction that we can be at all sure that American poetic genius has struck its native note. Therefore it becomes appropriate and important that this collection of American Indian verse should be brought to public notice at a time when the whole instinctive movement of the American people is for a deeper footing in their native soil. It is the certificate of our adoption, that the young genius of our time should strike all unconsciously on this ancient track to the High Places. (*MASW*, 192)

The connection between place and poetry is universal, but it is also intensely local. For that reason, Austin insists on a literary nationalism that realizes the "deeper footing" of indigenous poetry in native soil. The journey to authentic poetry, in whatever age, must travel the "ancient track to the High Places."

The introduction to *Path on the Rainbow* makes important claims for Native American poetry in several ways. Partly, Austin uses the authoritative tone of an anthropologist or literary critic to make large assertions concerning the relationship between ancient and modern American verse forms. She also delineates characteristics of Amerindian poetry that establish its unique quality and inherent value. These two aspects of the introduction often appear side by side. For example, Austin imagines pre-Columbian poetic art as having "reached a mark close to that of the Greeks at the beginning of the Homeric era," and she moves from that broad claim to more precise ones, asserting that in Native American cultures "neither poetry nor drama were yet divorced from singing, and all art was but half-born out of the Great Mystery" (*MASW*, 192). In a characteristic metaphor, Austin presents the merging of dance, song, and poetry in terms of landscape: "Words, melody and movement were as much mixed as the water of a river with its own ripples and its rate of flowing" (192). Other important traits of Native American poetry are its mnemonic power and its ritual functions, both of which suggest the fundamental role of art in the life of a community. According to Austin, Amerindian poems are "songs for occasions," and there are "songs for every possible adventure of tribal life; songs for setting out on a journey, a song for the first sight of your destination, and a song to be sung by your wife for your safe return" (193).

Perhaps the most important aspect of Amerindian poetry, in Austin's view, is its "magic power" (192). She explains this point by appealing to Native American cosmology: "Tirawa, Wokonda, The Friend of the Soul of Man, is in everything; in the field we plant, the stone we grind with, the bear we kill. By singing, the soul of the singer is put in harmony with the essential Essence of Things" (192–93). Poetry, seen in this way, is "the Path on the Rainbow by which the soul climbs; it lays hold on the Friend of the Soul of Man. Such exalted states are held to be protective and curative. Medicine men sing for their patients, and, in times of war, wives gather around the Chief's woman and sing for the success of their warriors" (194). The "Path on the Rainbow" echoes the phrases "the road to the spring" and the "ancient track to the High Places," and all three images of journeys suggest that poetry takes its participants—both poet and audience, both singer and community—toward a higher or deeper plane of spiritual knowledge and power.

The most controversial review of *The Path on the Rainbow* appeared in the *Dial* on March 8, 1919. In an essay titled "The Indian as Poet," the New York critic Louis Untermeyer mixed praise and blame for *The Path on the Rainbow.* He referred to Austin's "illuminating introduction" at the same time that he voiced his doubts concerning Cronyn's "hybrid if not actually dubious offspring." He mocked the modernist typography of several poems, calling them "odd-shaped pieces of sentimentality," but then he admitted that Austin had already met part of his objection when she asserted ironically that the reader "may, if he happens to be of the Imagist's party, suffer a check in the discovery that the first free movement of poetic originality in America finds us just about where the last Medicine Man left off" (*MASW*, 191).[3]

In a May 31, 1919, letter to the editor of the *Dial*, Austin responded in detail to Untermeyer's review. Not only does her letter question Untermeyer's ability to judge the value of the anthology; it also answers his specific objections point by point. In taking up the reviewer's examples of "odd-shaped" sentimental poems, for example, Austin adopts the tone of a cultural critic: "What must always be taken into consideration behind Indian songs is democracy of thinking and feeling. The communal life of the Indian leads to a community of thinking which made many words unnecessary, made the words a spring for the release of emotion which might be anything but banal" (*MASW*, 199–200). She adds several more important points when she remarks, "If Mr. Untermeyer could get his mind off the Indian Anthology as a thing of type and paper, he might have got something more out of it. . . . No one who reads the Hako ceremony of the Pawnees, realizing that the Pawnee country

3. Louis Untermeyer, "The Indian as Poet," *Dial*, March 8, 1919, 240.

is open, rolling prairie, lifting toward long level mesas, can fail to be struck with the way in which the shape of the lines is influenced by the contours of the country. It was in order to show just such local influences that the poems in the Anthology were grouped sectionally rather than tribally" (200).

The specific relationship of the "shape of the lines" to the "contours of the country" may not be perfectly clear in the Hako ceremony of the Pawnee, but Austin clearly evokes the powerful influence of the landscape on cultural forms. In fact, several parts of the eighteen rituals reproduced in the Hako ceremony appeal strongly to the landscape itself. In the fifth ritual, for instance, several long-lined songs evoke the sacred journey of the Pawnee as they follow Mother Corn, and they do so by focusing on aspects of the land: "Song to the Trees and Streams," "Song When Crossing the Streams," "Song to the Mountains," "Song to the Mesa."[4] In addition, the regional arrangement of the songs in the first part of *The Path on the Rainbow* supports ecocritical interpretations of the relationship between landscape and culture. The anthology presents the Indian songs in seven sections, traveling from Eastern Woodlands to the Southeast, across the Great Plains to the Southwest and California, then up the Northwest coast to the Far North. The movement of the sections cleverly mimics the history of contact between European settlers and Native peoples, and it also mimics the east-to-west expanse of the American continent. Without exaggerating the importance of the arrangement, Austin rightly notes that Untermeyer missed that point completely.

Recent scholars of Austin's work have refined and enriched the sense of her regionalism. Heike Schaefer's *Mary Austin's Regionalism* (2004) is a thorough, nuanced account of the prose works for

4. The Hako Ceremony is "rendered in the rhythms of the originals" by Alice Fletcher, who also published her translations as "The Hako, A Pawnee Ceremony," *Twenty-second Annual Report of the Bureau of American Ethnology* (Washington, D.C.: Smithsonian Institution, 1904). See Castro 19–25, for a helpful discussion of the anthology and its critics.

which Austin is best known. Schaefer argues that Austin manages to avoid the pitfalls of "geographical determination" and the postmodern divorce of language from reality by gesturing in both directions without declaring absolute allegiance to either. By focusing on the processes of individual identity formation and the environment, Schaefer portrays Austin as a pluralistic thinker who looks forward, in numerous ways, to current discussions of environmental literature, feminism, religion and ecology, and sustainability.[5]

Austin's relationship with the New York literary establishment was not always so vexed as the exchange with Untermeyer suggests. For example, the critic Carl Van Doren asked her to write a chapter, "Aboriginal Non-English Writings," for his *Cambridge History of American Literature* (1921).[6] As Karen Langlois points out, in the 1920s Austin "kept her name before the public with a steady stream of articles and book reviews about indigenous American culture. There was growing popular interest in the subject of Native Americans, and Austin was indefatigable in persuading editors to accept her expertise on practically every aspect of primitive life and to give her space in their periodicals."[7] Just three years after the exchange with Untermeyer, on the evening of January 8, 1922, literary New York gathered at the National Arts Club to honor her with a formal dinner and a round of laudatory speeches. The occasion was Austin's imminent departure for Santa Fe, New Mexico, where she would live for the last decade of her life. Henry Seidel Canby, editor of the *Literary Review* of the *New York Evening Post*, rose to toast her as "the one complete master of the American Environment," and Austin demonstrated her mastery by delivering a speech titled "American

5. Heike Schaefer, *Mary Austin's Regionalism: Reflections on Gender, Genre, and Geography* (Charlottesville: University of Virginia Press, 2004). See especially 1–84.

6. See Karen S. Langlois, "Marketing the American Indian: Mary Austin and the Business of Writing," *A Living of Words: American Women in Print Culture*, ed. Susan Albertine (Knoxville: University of Tennessee Press, 1995), 151–68.

7. Langlois, 158.

Literature as an Expression of the American Experience."[8] Austin outlined the ideas she developed most fully in the introduction to *The American Rhythm*, which she would publish just over a year later.

In Search of an American Rhythm

The introduction to *The American Rhythm* (1923) both summarizes and develops characteristic principles of Austin's poetics. The thesis of the long, formal essay, for instance, echoes the title of Austin's 1922 dinner address: "American poetry must inevitably take, at some period of its history, the mold of Amerind verse, which is the mold of the American experience shaped by the American environment."[9] In developing her argument, Austin develops an intriguing mixture of tones and styles. In the opening pages, she adopts a quasi-scientific style: "Rhythm, then, in so far as it affects our poetic mode, has nothing to do with our intellectual life. It is located in the dimension of appreciable stress. Its measure is the measure of the capacity of opposing organic strains" (*AR*, 4). The tone is unintentionally ironic, resulting from Austin's pedantic attempts to give scientific authority to her insights concerning poetry and the environment. Austin merges psychology and anthropology in several parts of the introduction. In section III, for example, she attempts to describe the "Dawn Mind" of the "Dawn Man," figuring Native Americans as psychologically complex and perceptually well-endowed: "The Indian sees no better than the white man, but he sees more, registers through every sense, some of which have atrophied in us, infinitely more. It is upon this enlarged reservoir of sensory impressions that he draws in his poetic

8. For an account of the dinner, see Esther Lanigan Stineman, *Mary Austin: Song of a Maverick* (New Haven: Yale University Press, 1989), 123–26. See also the description of Austin's costume and her Chickasaw escort in Langlois, 160, and in Susan Goodman and Carl Dawson, *Mary Austin and the American West* (Berkeley: University of California Press, 2008), 172–73.

9. *The American Rhythm* (New York: Harcourt, Brace 1923), 42. Hereafter cited parenthetically as AR.

dance dramas, every one of which comprises an orchestration of subjectively coordinated rhythms which the white man cannot always perceive and not easily resolve into mathematical indices" (*AR*, 29).[10]

Despite passages that sometimes plunge toward ethnocentrism, or even racism, Austin often argues persuasively for the role of the environment in shaping cultural productions. In a telling example, her discussion of the American landscape in relation to American history leads her to remark on a personal discovery concerning the rhythms of her own prose:

> Only a few months ago, when I had occasion to turn back to one of my desert books, written eighteen years ago and scarcely looked at since, I discovered the first paragraph striking without intention into the irregular tug and release of the four-horse Mojave stage and of the eighteen-mule borax team, from which my association with the scenes described was almost never freed. Probably the deep self from which poetry springs picks up a new rhythm very quickly when there is little or no expenditure of physical energy, and the psyche is free to concern itself with wonder and delight. (*AR*, 14–15)

Here the psychology of intention and association arises from Austin's own personal experience, and for that reason the "deep self" she describes has persuasive power. The speculations about physical energy and the psyche's capacity for wonder and delight are intriguing because they are not burdened with pseudo-authority. On the other hand, for many readers, the subjective quality of Austin's assertions may undercut their validity. The specific images of horse and

10. For two excellent recent discussions of Austin's view of Native American cultures, see Schaefer 146–77, and Noreen Groover Lape, "'There was a part for her in the Indian life': Mary Austin, Regionalism, and the Problems of Appropriation," in *Breaking Boundaries: New Perspectives on Women's Regional Writing*, ed. Sherrie A. Inness and Diana Royer (Iowa City: University of Iowa Press, 1997), 124–39.

mule teams, moreover, are difficult to connect to any specific prose rhythms in Austin's writing. In the first paragraphs of her first two desert books, *The Land of Little Rain* (1903) and *The Flock* (1906), Austin does not specifically evoke the imagery of such teams, but she does create a rhythmical prose style through repetition and parallel syntax. There are images of horses, sheep, and human beings moving across the landscape—true, too, in the opening paragraph of Austin's first novel, *Isidro* (1905)—but the style evokes the panorama of the desert rather than any "tug and release" movement of horses or mules in harness. Indeed, in the opening of *The Land of Little Rain*, Austin remarks that "Desert is a loose term to indicate land that supports no man; whether the land can be bitted and broken to that purpose is not proven."[11] How the land can be "bitted and broken" to the purpose of poetry remains an open question as well.

The deep cultural power of rhythmical possibilities comes out fully in "Hasta Mañana," the prophetic concluding chapter to Austin's second nonfiction book about the desert, *Land of Journeys' Ending* (1924). As in the other books about the Southwest, Austin focuses on the central "working relationship" between the land and its inhabitants:

> Man is not himself only, not solely a variation of his racial type in the pattern of his immediate experience. He is all that he sees; all that flows to him from a thousand sources, half noted, or noted not at all except by some sense that lies too deep for naming. He is the land, the lift of its mountain lines, the reach of its valleys; his is the rhythm of its seasonal processions, the involution and variation of its vegetal patterns. If there is in the country of his abiding, no more than a single refluent color, such as the veiled green of sage-brush or the splendid wine of sunset spilled along the Sangre de Cristo, he takes it in and gives it forth again in directions and

11. *Stories from the Country of Lost Borders*, ed. Marjorie Pryse (New Brunswick, NJ: Rutgers University Press, 1987), 9.

> occasions least suspected by himself, as a manner, as music, as a prevailing tone of thought, as the line of his roof-tree, the pattern of his personal adornment.[12]

The long process by which the rhythms of the land become part of the inhabitants seems effortless in this passage, as if it could not be otherwise. But Austin recognizes that cultural expressions develop slowly and that they depend "on the realization and general adoption of native symbols for experiences intimate and peculiar to that land. The profoundest implications of human experience are never stated rationally, never with explicitness, but indirectly in what we agree to call art forms, rhythms, festivals, designs, melodies, objective symbolic substitutions" (*LJE*, 440).

Austin's poetic theory enacts, indirectly and subtly, the "opposing organic strains" and "tug and release" that form the basic principle she sees in the American rhythm. In section 2 of the *American Rhythm* introduction, for example, in which she discusses the rhythms of harnessed teams, she insists on the physical aspects of American frontier history by evoking ways in which the "rhythm of walking, always a recognizable background for our thoughts, altered from the militaristic stride to the jog of the wide, unrutted earth. Explorer, fur-trader, King's agent, whoever for three centuries followed it, must have carried a record of its foot work in his walk, a wider swing and recovery to his mind" (*AR*, 14). According to Austin's history, the "heritage of rhythms" should have been based on "the tug and heave of constructive labor," but the academic and intellectual caste put the educated young through other paces. Despite such "carpet-treading," however, even an educated poet like Ralph Waldo Emerson could not escape the American landscape: "Emerson came stumbling into the American trail about Monadnoc" (15).

12. *The Land of Journeys' Ending* (New York: Century, 1924); rpt., with an introduction by Melody Graulich (Urbana: University of Illinois Press, 2003), 437. Hereafter cited parenthetically as LJE.

Austin finds the most authentic American rhythms in two icons of the "wilderness track," Whitman's "Song of the Open Road" and Abraham Lincoln's Gettysburg Address (15–18). In both Whitman and Lincoln, Austin praises what she calls "the urge and recovery of the democratic experience" (18), a double experience that clearly parallels the dual rhythmical movement of tug and release. For readers more accustomed to the language of traditional metrics, Austin's dualisms could evoke stressed and unstressed syllables.

If the wilderness provides Austin with a democratic, oppositional, "frontier" model for poetic rhythms, she finds a far more powerful model in the indigenous Native American communities:

> All this time there was an American race singing in tune with the beloved environment, to the measures of life-sustaining gestures, taking the material of their songs out of the common human occasions, out of the democratic experience and the profound desire of man to assimilate himself to the Allness as it is displayed to him in all the peacock splendor of the American continent. In so far as verse forms are shaped by topography and the rhythm of food supply, the aboriginal American was singing in precisely the forms that were later to become native to the region of Spoon River, the Land of Little Rain, and the country of the Cornhuskers. (18–19)

In the last sentence, Austin alludes to works by Edgar Lee Masters, herself, and Carl Sandburg, crossing the genres of poetry and nonfiction prose. The crossing of genre boundaries parallels the ways in which rhythm as a concept crosses from "food supply" to "the measures of life-sustaining gestures." For Austin, Amerindian song embodies the rhythms of landscape, the working relationships of human communities with the lands they inhabit, and the religious rituals that make those rhythms and relationships sacred. The introduction to the 1923 edition of *The American Rhythm* argues both implicitly and explicitly that Amerindian song reveals the "road to the spring" for modern American literature, and that some writers in the West have already followed that path (*AR*, 50). At various points in the introduction, Austin names particular modern poets as working toward the spring of "native inspiration." She cites Carl Sandburg, Vachel Lindsay, and Sherwood Anderson as heirs apparent to Walt Whitman (32–33). Amy Lowell, Sandburg, Lindsay, and Edgar Lee Masters unconsciously echo the rhythms of the American environment and indigenous songs (45–46). Stephen Crane is somehow able to approach "nearer the poetic modes of the Rio Grande country than any white man has been since" (53). Finally, Masters, Robert Frost, and Sandburg struggle toward the sense of community and communion that Native Americans have developed through "easy evolution" (54).

As recent scholars have pointed out, Austin's authority concerning the relationship between ancient and modern American cultures did not go unquestioned. In 1922, for example, Austin conducted a public dispute with Alice Corbin Henderson, the associate editor of *Poetry* magazine, concerning the term *Amerindian* and the path from Native American rhythms to modernist poetry. Writing to the *Chicago Daily News*, Austin defended her use of the term and then hedged her argument: "I am not an authority on any phase of Indian life. I have made use of what I have learned from my study of the American Indian in certain other fields in which I also have some reason to speak if not with authority, at least more freely than other American writers. Outside of these special subjects—poetic rhythm is one of them—I leave the questions of terms to authoritative workers in that field. And Mrs. Henderson is not one of them."[13] Even if Austin were correct about Henderson's authority, she freely admits in *The American Rhythm* that several ethnologists have questioned her work. At the very end of the introduction to the 1923 edition, she acknowledges the work of eight scholars of Native American culture and adds, "Though they do not always take me so seriously as I take

13. Quoted in Goodman and Dawson, *Mary Austin and the American West*, 200. Goodman and Dawson give the most definitive discussion of Austin's career to date.

them, it would be unfair not to admit that they always take me good-humoredly. That I should make mistakes in a field where so little had been done before me was to have been expected. That the only mistake I have ever had publicly to correct came of my trusting to the ethnologists too implicitly is my excuse for occasionally venturing beyond their findings on ground where nobody but a poet could have ventured at all" (*AR*, 65).

In tracing the paths between modern American poets and Amerindian song, Austin uses two evocative descriptive terms: *landscape line* and *glyph*. The first term concisely recalls Austin's statement about the Hako ceremony in the 1919 letter to the *Dial*: "the shape of the lines is influenced by the contours of the country" (*MASW*, 200). But Austin gives other definitions of the "landscape line" that render its meaning ambiguous. In *The American Rhythm*, she calls it "the line shaped by its own inner necessities" (*AR*, 54) and distinguishes it from the "melodic line," which Amerindian song creates by "repetitions of felicitous phrases or by sheer meaningless syllabication, rather than force the meaning with added words, as our classic poets are obliged to do, or to pad it with adjectives until it fills out every accent of the musical measure" (55). The "melodic line" resembles the metrical frame of traditional accentual-syllabic verse, providing a coherent structure for the song or poem. But Austin insists that such a "predetermined mold" is rare in Amerindian verse:

> Mold or rhythm-pattern, so far as it exists for the aboriginal exists only as a point of rest for the verse to flow into and out of as a mountain stream flows in and out of ripple-linked pools. It is this leap of the running stream of poetic inspiration from level to level, whose course cannot be determined by anything except the nature of the ground traversed, which I have called the landscape line. (*AR*, 55)

Clarifying the metaphor of the mountain stream, Austin compares the Amerindian landscape line to the modern printed poem. The landscape line can in fact appear in print as several verse lines "and is best described by the modern term, cadenced verse. In the placing of this line, and the additional items by which it is connotated and decorated, the aboriginal process approaches closest to what is known as Imagism, unless you will accept my term and call it glyphic" (*AR*, 56). The "landscape line" emerges, then, as cadenced verse, without predetermined length or metrical frame. The form is determined by the writer's inspiration and by the occasion, "the nature of the ground traversed."

If the landscape line is a particular version of free verse, whose cadences are somehow influenced by the contours of the country, the term *glyph* suggests the more visual term *image* as defined by Ezra Pound in the March 1913 issue of *Poetry*: "that which presents an intellectual and emotional complex in an instant of time."[14] Austin uses visual examples to define the term *glyph*, which in fact refers to visual images incised on stone, as in petroglyphs or hieroglyphs. The best example, however, comes from the cover design of the 1923 edition of *The American Rhythm*, where the glyph is an abstract representation enclosed within a circular borderline. According to Austin, the glyph figures an abstract Thunderbird, "reproduced from a ceremonial bowl unearthed in one of the pre-Columbian pueblos. Within the circle fixed by the bowl's proportions, we have not a drawing of a bird, but an adequate suggestion of birdness, of birdness the most majestic, whose wings are made of the dark cloud, whose feathers are edged with the dark mist, presiding over fertility provoking storms, and hence also the presiding genius of power-inducing song" (*AR*,

14. The March 1913 issue of *Poetry* contains Pound's famous three-part Imagist principles. My discussion has been aided greatly by James Ruppert, "Discovering America: Mary Austin and Imagism," in *Studies in American Indian Literature: Critical Essays and Course Designs*, ed. Paula Gunn Allen (New York: Modern Language Association of America, 1983), 243–58. Ruppert asserts that the landscape line "coheres to the third principle of Imagism: it is composed in the sequence of the musical phrase as opposed to stiffly defined metrics" (253). My reading of the term in relation to the "contours of the country" and in opposition to the "melodic line" suggests a place-based interpretation.

51–52). Austin gives examples of glyphs in three poems—one called "The Magic Ribbon," by Washoe Charlie, and the other two from Stephen Crane's *The Black Riders and Other Lines* (1895). All these examples lead to the sense of the glyph as a visual image, a fragmentary and momentary experience expressed as concisely as possible. Or, as Austin puts it, the glyph is "a type of Amerind song which is lyric in its emotional quality and yet cannot be completely expressed by the simple lyric cry" (*AR*, 53).[15] In addition, the word specifically connotes Pueblo religious carvings, used to signify important relationships in Pueblo worship.[16]

The critical response to *The American Rhythm* was not uniformly enthusiastic, but two prominent reviews from 1923 were overwhelmingly positive. In a four-paragraph essay in the *Nation*, Mark Van Doren portrays Austin as a "true mystic" whose effort to translate her vision into words "is not wholly successful" but "impressive, and though it is not convincing it is great." Van Doren ultimately urges caution in responding to Austin's prophetic call for a new poetry, for he finds her demands "ruthless." Still, he ends the review by emphasizing Austin's importance: "She has issued a challenge which will make every honest American poet stop to examine himself. And that is an excellent thing."[17]

Carl Van Doren's essay in the November 1923 issue of *Century* magazine gives an expansive account of Austin's career. Subtitled "Mary Austin: Discoverer and Prophet," the essay places Austin's

15. Ruppert suggestively associates the glyph with the Chinese ideogram, though he does not develop the connection to Pound and Ernest Fenollosa's "Essay on the Chinese Written Character," 253–55.

16. Elsie Clew Parsons, *The Pueblo Indian Religion* (Chicago: University of Chicago Press, 1939), 1: 353–60.

17. Castro summarizes the response to *Path on the Rainbow* and *The American Rhythm*, focusing especially on the exchange of letters in the pages of the *Dial* in 1919 (42–45). The one completely negative review is by Lewis Mumford, in the *New Republic*, May 30, 1923, 23–24. All quotations in my paragraph are from Mark Van Doren, "The American Rhythm," *Nation*, April 18, 1923, 472.

poetic work in the context of American cultural history, locating her career within the search for an indigenous idiom, "some common ground for the American philosopher or artist to stand upon." Van Doren especially admires Austin's desert books, but he asserts that "her conception of landscape and climate touches all she writes." He portrays her as a desert prophet: "She speaks as if she had just come back from the desert with fresh truth. But the desert from which she has come is not in California; it is in the clear country of the mind. The temptation is to say that the region lies deeper: in the soul, perhaps, or in the memory of the race." Moreover, according to Van Doren, Austin must be judged as a prophet and poet, and she stands the test well: "A decade before the newer forms of verse came into fashion, she had forecast them and practiced them, deriving her methods from those of the primitive Americans near whom she lived." While Van Doren finds Austin's art less successful than her prophecy, he praises her critical writings and "those lovely, luminous documents on the Southwest."[18]

Despite the steady stream of publications and positive reviews in major periodicals across the country, Austin would write in her autobiography, *Earth Horizon*, that "there was a general withdrawal of interest in the subject of Indian poetry, an unwillingness to give it attention. There was an indisposition to admit it to discussion, especially on the basis on which I had introduced it. Most of the reviewers took it for granted that I had said that American poetry was derived from Indian, and scoffed at the idea."[19] Ever persistent, Austin was just beginning to develop her sense of landscape in poetry. In 1922, after her farewell dinner at the National Arts Club, Austin moved to Santa Fe, New Mexico, throwing herself into the landscape and culture of the Pueblo and Navajo Indians. She continued to write poems

18. Carl Van Doren, "The American Rhythm. Mary Austin: Discoverer and Prophet," *Century*, November 1923, 151–56.

19. Mary Austin, *Earth Horizon: Autobiography* (Boston: Houghton Mifflin, 1932), 345.

in free verse, many of which took on the mythological themes and ceremonial forms of Amerindian and colonial Spanish traditions. She continued to publish poems in major periodicals, both in New York City and in the Southwest. And she continued to champion indigenous cultural practices in the Southwest.[20]

The present edition of Austin's collected poems retrieves a missing part of her legacy as a writer. In all of her poems, even the earliest efforts, Austin develops a rich, deep sense of place, and she ranges widely across a host of places. Amerindian songs and belief systems exercise an abiding, strong influence on Austin's style and subject matter, forming a critical aspect of her literary topography. Tellingly, at one time Austin planned to name the 1923 edition of *The American Rhythm* with one of her favorite images: *The Road to the Spring*. She decided against the title, though she used the image in the 1923 introduction and in the 1926 article in the *Nation*: "It is the road to the spring that we travel, to the source of man's medium, rather than to his emotions; a road which every people must take from time to time if it would not see its own most intimate expression smothered in staleness, ossified by tradition." Every poem is a version of the road, and in every poem Mary Austin takes a step toward the spring of new inspiration. In a writing career of forty years, she took many roads to many springs. Now we have them for a fresh journey.

20. For this last period in her life, see Goodman and Dawson 172–263.

BOOK PUBLICATIONS

The American Rhythm, 1923

The 1923 edition of *The American Rhythm* presents an intriguing mixture of texts. Austin's long introduction is of great interest as an essay in poetics, connecting environmental, ethnic, and formal concerns. The first section of poems, "Amerindian Songs (Re-expressed from the Originals)," includes twenty-three titles, many of which are love lyrics. Only a few of these "re-expressions" are directly connected to rituals or ceremonies, though Austin is careful to cite the names of the tribes with which she associates the poems. As she states toward the end of her introduction to *The Path on the Rainbow*, it seems that Austin's aim in the first section is "feeling rather for a full expression of Indian thought, than for lyric quality," and while she claims that "the long divided Muses of poetry, music and dance must come together again for the absolute rendering," her own re-expressions do not fully attempt that three-part poetic union (xxxi).

The last section of *The American Rhythm*, "Songs in the American Manner," includes nineteen of Austin's original poems, but only one or two evoke Amerindian songs in style or form. All are free-verse poems, in the general sense that they employ no metric scheme and use typography and repetition as the basic means of establishing a rhythmic pattern. Several focus on a specific image, presenting that moment in time and perception in a way we can call imagist or glyphic, but several others are discursive and diffuse. From 1917 to 1923, Austin had published ten of the poems in *Poetry*, Harriet Monroe's new magazine for the very best modern verse. Other poems had appeared in *Bookman*, *Harper's*, *Harper's Weekly*, *McClure's*, and *Forum*, as well as in smaller-circulation magazines. The organization of the book suggests a connection between the ancient poetry of American Indians and the modern free verse of Americans like Austin herself. Moreover, in the 1923 "Songs in the American Manner," Austin boldly explores modern themes of feminism and pacifism through a variety of experiments in free verse. Readers of *The Land of Little Rain* (1903) will have little difficulty in seeing Austin's role as an early ecofeminist and regionalist.

Amerindian Songs Re-expressed from the Originals

Heart's Friend

Fair is the white star of twilight
And the sky clearer
At the day's end;
But she is fairer,
And she is dearer,
She, my heart's friend!

Fair is the white star of twilight
And the moon roving
To the sky's end;
But she is fairer,
And she is dearer,
She, my heart's friend!

From the Paiute.

Editor's Notes

Austin titles the poem "The Heart's Friend (Shoshone Love Song)" in *The Path on the Rainbow* 223.

The Grass on the Mountain

Oh, long, long
The snow has possessed the mountains.

The deer have come down and the big-horn,
They have followed the Sun to the south
To feed on the mesquite pods and the bunch grass.
Loud are the thunder drums
In the tents of the mountains.

Oh, long, long
Have we eaten chia seeds
And dried deer's flesh of the summer killing.
We are wearied of our huts
And the smoky smell of our garments.

We are sick with desire of the sun
And the grass on the mountain.

From the Paiute.

Editor's Notes

Published in *Poetry* 15 (January 1920): 182-83.

The chia plant, Salvia hispanica, produces seeds used for porridge and was a staple of Native Americans in the Southwest.

Song for the Passing of a Beautiful Woman

Strong sun across the sod can make
Such quickening as your countenance!

I am more worth for what your passing wakes,
Great races in my loins, to you that cry.
My blood is redder for your loveliness.

From the Paiute.

Song for the Passing of Beautiful Women (From the Paiute)

Go thy way in comeliness!
Strong sun across the sod doth make
Such quickening as thy countenance.

Pursue thy unguessed errand and pass by;
I am more worth for what thy passing wakes,
Great races in my loins to thee that cry!
My blood is redder for thy loveliness.
Prosper; be fair; pass by!

Editor's Notes

Path on the Rainbow 222

Song for the Newborn

To be sung by the one who first takes the child from its mother.

Newborn, on the naked sand
Nakedly lay it.
Next to the earth mother,
That it may know her;
Having good thoughts of her, the food giver.

Newborn, we tenderly
In our arms take it,
Making good thoughts.
House-god, be entreated,
That it may grow from childhood to manhood,
Happy, contented;
Beautifully walking
The trail to old age.
Having good thoughts of the earth its mother,
That she may give it the fruits of her being.
Newborn, on the naked sand
Nakedly lay it.

Grande Pueblos.

Editor's Notes

Published in *Harper's*, June 1921.

The Rio Grande Pueblos live along the Rio Grande River northeast of Santa Fe, New Mexico.

Warrior's Song

Weep not for me, Loved Woman,
Should I die;
But for yourself be weeping!

Weep not for warriors who go
Gladly to battle.
Theirs to revenge
Fallen and slain of our people;
Theirs to lay low
All our foes like them,
Death to make, singing.

Weep not for warriors,
But weep for women!
Oh, weep for all women!

Theirs to be pitied
Most of all creatures,
Whose men return not!
How shall their hearts be stayed
When we are fallen?

Weep not for me, Loved Woman,
For yourself alone be weeping!

The Eagle's Song

Said the Eagle:
I was astonished
When I heard that there was death.

My home, alas,
Must I leave it!
All beholding summits,
Shall I see thee no more!

North I went,
Leaning on the wind;
Through the forest resounded
The cry of the hunted doe.

East I went,
Through the hot dawning;
There was the smell of death in my nostrils.

South I went, seeking
The place where there is no death.
Weeping I heard
The voice of women
Wailing for their children.

West I went,
On the world-encompassing water;
Death's trail was before me.

People, O people,
Needs be that we must die!

Therefore let us make
Songs together.

With a twine of songs to bind us
To the middle Heaven,
The white way of souls.
There we shall be at rest,
With our songs
We shall roam no more!

Southern California.

Editor's Notes

Published in *Poetry*, January 1920, 181–82.

Young Men's Song

Ah--ahou! Ahou--aou!*
Hi! Hi! Hi! Hi-ah-ee--ah!

Go we now,
        Go we now,
                Go . . o . . o now!
Ahou! Ahou! Ahou! Ahou!

Go we where the trail leads,
        It leads before us!

Ahou . . aou . . aou . . aou . . aou . . aou!+
Ai . . ai . . ai . . ai . . ai . . ai!
Go we
        Go we
                Go . . o . . o now!
Many scalps
We shall bring returning.

Go we
                Ahou!
                                Ahou!
Hi! Hi! Hi!
Ai . . ai . . ai . . ai . . ai . . ai . . i . . ee!

*Call to attract the attention of War god.
+ Prolong by clapping hand on mouth.

Editor's Notes

Reprinted in *Children Sing in the Far West* (1928).

Woman's Song

These are the First Born
Of the First People.
Topal, the grinding stone,
Kenhut, the wampum string,
Paviut, the knife.

When the Empty Quietness
Begot the Engendering Mist,
Then came the Sky Man,
Came the Earth Mother,
Who made the Grinding Stone,
Who made the Hunting Knife,
Who made the Wampum String.

Thus runs the song around,
Under what tribal change soe'er you find them.
Where there are women found
There sits the grinding stone;
Where there arc men
There glints the hunting knife;
Where there are People
There goes the wampum string.
Thus runs the song around.

From the Luiseño.

Editor's Notes

Published in *Harper's*, June 1921, 78.

The Luiseño lived on the California coast from southern Los Angeles County to San Diego. They were named by the Spanish after the Mission of San Luis Rey de Francia in the eighteenth century.

The three terms in the first stanza refer both to sacred objects and to the names of the First People they represent; see Constance

Goddard DuBois, "Religion of the Luiseño Indians," *American Archaeology and Ethnology* 8, no. 3 (June 27, 1908): 130.

A Song in Depression

Now all my singing dreams are gone!
None knows where they have fled
Nor by what trails they have left me.

Return, O dreams of my heart,
And sing in the summer twilight,
By the creek and the almond thicket
And the field that is bordered with lupines.

Now is my refuge to seek
In the hollow of friendly shoulders,
Since the singing is stopped in my pulse
And the earth and the sky refuse me.
Now must I hold by the eyes of a friend
When the high white stars are unfriendly.

Over-sweet is the refuge for trusting.
Return and sing, O my Dreams,
In the dewy and palpitant pastures,
Till the love of living awakes
And the strength of the hills to uphold me!

From the Washoe-Paiute.

Editor's Notes

Published as "A Song in Time of Depression" in *Everybody's Magazine*, 31 (1914): 413–15 and reprinted in *Path on the Rainbow* 223–24.

Washoe and Northern Paiute are neighboring tribes of eastern California and the Great Basin of Nevada. Culturally and linguistically distinct from one another, they were often at war.

Sioux Song at Parting

Breaks now, breaks now my heart,
Thinking, from thee I part.
Hear thou what says my heart:
Keep me,
Keep me in thine alway!

Dreams now, dreams now my heart.
Weeping, awake I start,
Thinking, again we part.
Dream thou,
Perchance thy dream will stay!

The Yielding Heart

Too soon I yield, I fear,
Too soon!
Yet yielding I rejoice
That in your touch
Such power should be,
Such magic in your voice!

From the Yokut.

Editor's Notes

The Yokut comprise over sixty distinct tribes in central and northern California; they are now better known as the Mariposa.

Come Not Near My Songs

Come not near my songs,
You who are not my lover,
Lest from out that ambush
Leaps my heart upon you!

When my songs are glowing
As an almond thicket
With the bloom upon it,
Lies my heart in ambush
All amid my singing;
Come not near my songs,
You who are not my lover!

Do not hear my songs,
You who are not my lover!
Over-sweet the heart is,
Where my love has bruised it,
Breathe you not that fragrance,
You who are not my lover.
Do not stoop above my song,
With its languor on you,
Lest from out my singing
Leaps my heart upon you!

From the Shoshone.

Editor's Notes

The Shoshone are a tribe with three large divisions—Northern, Eastern, and Western. The Western Shoshone occupied Panamint Valley and Death Valley in California.

Song of the Basket Dancers

I

We, the Rain Cloud callers,
Ancient mothers of the Rain Cloud clan,
Basket bearers;
We entreat you,
O ye Ancients,
By the full-shaped womb,
That the lightning and the thunder and the rain
Shall come upon the earth,
Shall fructify the earth;
That the great rain clouds shall come upon the earth
As the lover to the maid.

II

Send your breath to blow the clouds,
O ye Ancients,
As the wind blows the plumes
Of our eagle-feathered prayer sticks,
Send, O ye Ancients,
To the Six Corn Maidens.
To the White Corn Maiden,
To the Yellow Corn Maiden,
To the Red Corn Maiden,
To the Blue Corn Maiden,
To the Many Colored Maiden
To the Black Corn Maiden,
That their wombs bear fruit.

III

Let the thunder be heard,
O ye Ancients!
Let the sky be covered with white blossom clouds,
That the earth, O ye Ancients,
Be covered with many colored flowers.
That the seeds come up,
That the stalks grow strong
That the people have corn,
That happily they eat.
Let the people have corn to complete the road of life.

Editor's Notes

Austin's note 13 states that an interpreter gave her these three songs from San Ildefonso Pueblo, near Santa Fe. The basket dances were a harvest and fertility ritual performed by women's societies among Hopi, Tewa, and Jemez pueblos; weather ceremonies also figured in such dances, as do the mythological figures of the Corn Maidens. See Elsie Clews Parsons's extensive discussion of ceremonies in *Pueblo Indian Religion* 2: 551–860.

Lament of a Man for his Son

Son, my son!

I will go up to the mountain
And there I will light a fire
To the feet of my son's spirit,
And there will I lament him;
Saying,
O my son,
What is my life to me, now you are departed!

Son, my son,
In the deep earth
We softly laid thee in a Chief's robe,
In a warrior's gear.
Surely there,
In the spirit land
Thy deeds attend thee!
Surely,
The corn comes to the ear again!

But I, here,
I am the stalk that the seed-gatherers
Descrying empty, afar, left standing.
Son, my son!
What is my life to me, now you are departed?

Editor's Notes

Published in *Harper's*, June 1921, 79–80.

Medicine Songs

These are the songs of the Friend,
Made by the Medicine Man
In the young dusk of the Spring, moonless and tender.

At the hour when balm-giving herbs
Begin to be musky and sweet along the creek border,
When the smell of the sage is sharp in the trail of the cattle,
And the ants run busily still up the boles of the pine trees,
I heard the pound of his feet, and the roll of his ram's horn rattle.
Sweet was the drone of his song,
And the night desirous.

All night he sang,
Till the young, thin moon came up,
About the wolf hour of the morning.

The eyes of the Medicine Man
Were pale as the sloughs at sun-dawn.
The shadow of all his songs
Strewed the cheek hollows
Like ash in the pits of the hearthstone,
Bitter and thick was his voice
With the dust stirred up by his dancing.

These are the songs he made
To be sung for endurance of friendship,
Which still in my heart I hear
When I go by the sweet-smelling trails
In the moonless evenings of April.
My pulse is full of their whisper and beat,
Overfull and aching with song
And the roll of the ram's horn rattle,

When the smell of the camphire comes out by the creeks,
And the nights are young and desirous.

FIRST SONG

O winding trails that run out every way
To seek the happy places of the hills,
And stars that swirl about the hollow heaven,
You hear the rising of my songs
Like a morning full of wings.

O little trails, that whiten through the dunes,
A light is on you more than day has made.
And all my mind goes from me like a flame
To couple with the live thought of the world,
Because of this my friend.

SECOND SONG

What is this that stirs beside me
What sweet troubling?

It is my thought that quickens to my friend.
For my thought was as a woman
When her time is past and she bears no children.
Now the time returns
Tremulous and quick as my friend goes by me.

Now is my walking changed
And my strength braced with laughter.
I am so much more to myself
As the friend of my friend,
That the days shall not affront me,
Nor sighs, little sisters of pain, come nigh me.

THIRD SONG

Good is a maid in the hut
In the undark nights in summer
When her sides are slim and brown
And you prove her by her laughter.
But the love of man to man
Has mighty works to prove it.

FOURTH SONG

Lo, my heart is as a lair.
It is hidden under my songs,
And my dancing is a screen before its ways.

There my friend shall keep darkly,
When ill repute pursues him
There he shall lie safe
From malice and dishonor.

Editor's Notes

The introductory stanzas were published as "The Song of the Friend" in *McClure's*, January 1912, 351; the four songs were published in variant forms in *Harper's*, June 1921, 80.

Camphire is an alternative spelling of *camphor*, the aromatic substance derived from several kinds of plants, especially in Japan and China.

Papago Love Songs

I

Early I rose
In the blue morning;
My love was up before me,
It came running to me from the doorways of the Dawn.

On Papago Mountain
The dying quarry
Looked at me with my love's eyes.

II

Do you long, my Maiden,
For bisnaga blossoms
To fasten in your hair?

I will pick them for you.
What are bisnaga spines to me
Whom love is forever pricking in the side?

Editor's Notes

Papago is an earlier name for the Tohono O'odham tribe of the Sonoran desert in southwest Arizona and northern Mexico.

Bisnaga is an alternative term for barrel cactus, genus *Ferocactus*, taken from the Spanish term *viznaga*.

Glyphs

I

A girl wearing a green ribbon,—
As if it had been my girl.
—The green ribbon I gave her for remembrance—
Knowing all the time it was not my girl,
Such was the magic of that ribbon,
Suddenly,
My girl existed inside me!

II

Your face is strange,
And the smell of your garments,
But your soul is familiar;
As if in dreams our thoughts
Had visited one another.

Often from unremembering sleep
I wake delicately glowing.
Now I know what my heart has been doing.

Now I know why when we met
It slipped
So easily into loving.

III

Truly buzzards
Around my sky are circling!

For my soul festers,
And an odor of corruption
Betrays me to disaster.

Meanness, betrayal and spite
Come flockwise,
To make me aware
Of sickness and death within me.
My sky is full of the dreadful sound
Of the wings of unsuccesses.

From the Washoe-Paiute.

Editor's Notes

Glyphs I and II were published in reverse order in the *Dial*, November 1921, 555.

Glyphs

I

The Remembering Heart

Your face is strange
And the fashion of your garments.
But to me your soul is familiar,
As if in dreams our hearts
Had visited one another.

Often, from unremembering sleep I come
Delicately glowing.
Now I understand what my heart has been doing.

Now I know why, when I met you
It slipped
So easily into loving.

II

The Magic Ribbon

A girl wearing a green ribbon,
As if it had been my girl.
        (The green ribbon I gave her for remembrance)
Knowing all the time it was not my girl,
Suddenly
        (Such was the magic of the ribbon)
My girl existed inside me!

III

When I Think of My Beloved.

When I think of my beloved
When my heart is longing for her,

The yellow leaf bird in the corn is thinking too,
He is thinking with his music
He is longing with his singing.
When I think of my beloved
When my heart is longing for her.

Editor's Notes

AU 207: typescript with autograph corrections.

Glyphs IV

My days are full of the dreadful sound
Of the wings of unsuccesses.

For my soul festers
And an odor of corruption
Betrays me to disaster.

Meanness, betrayal and spite
Come flockwise
To make me aware
Of sickness and death within me.

Editor's Notes

AU 290.

Medicine Song

TO BE SUNG IN TIME OF EVIL FORTUNE
(From the Paiute Indian Dialect,
Done into English by Mary Austin)

Medicine me,
O Friend-of-the-Soul-of-Man,
With purging waters!
For my soul festers
And an odor of corruption
Betrays me to disaster.

As a place of carrion
Where buzzards are gathered,
So is my path
Overshadowed by evil adventures;
Meanness, betrayal, and spite
Flock under heaven
To make me aware
Of sickness and death within me.

Medicine my soul, O friend,
With waters of cleansing;
Then shall my way shine,
And my nights no longer
Be full of the dreadful sound
Of the wings of unsuccesses.

Editor's Notes

McClure's, September 1911, 504.

Neither Spirit nor Bird

Neither spirit nor bird;
That was my flute you heard
Last night by the river.
When you came with your wicker jar
Where the river drags the willows,
That was my flute you heard,
Wacoba, Wacoba,
Calling, Come to the willows!

Neither the wind nor a bird
Rustled the lupine blooms.
That was my blood you heard
Answer your garment's hem
Whispering through the grasses;
That was my blood you heard
By the wild rose under the willows.

That was no beast that stirred,
That was my heart you heard,
Pacing to and fro
In the ambush of my desire,
To the music my flute let fall.
Wacoba, Wacoba,
That was my heart you heard
Leaping under the willows.

From the Shoshone.

Editor's Notes

Published in *Poetry*, February 1917, 239, and in *Path on the Rainbow*, 220.

There is a Wacoba Pass near Inyo, California; no other use of the term has been found.

Rain Songs from the Rio Grande Pueblos

I

People of the middle heaven
Moving happily behind white floating cloud masks,
Moving busily behind rain-straitened cloud masks;
People of the Lightning,
People of the Thunder,
People of the Rainbow,
Rain! Rain! Rain!

II

Cloud priests,
Whose hearts ascend through the spruce tree
On the Mountains of the North,
                    Pray for us!
Cloud priests,
Whose hearts ascend
Through the pine of the West,
Through the oak of the South,
Through the aspen of the East,
Through the high-branched cedar of the zenith,
Through the low, dark cedar of the nadir,
                    Pray for us!

III

Archpriests of the six world quarters,
                    Work with us!
That the waters of the six great springs of the world
May fructify the Earth, our mother,
That she bring forth fruit for us!

We, the ancient ones,
From the four womb-worlds,
From the doorway of the underworld,
From Shipapu,
We, assembling,
Lifting up our thoughts to the clouds,
To the lightning, to the thunder,
Lifting up our hearts,
Make you precious medicine.

People of the Middle World,
Send your thoughts to us!
That our songs go straightly
On the sacred meal road,
The ancient road,
Walking it with power.
Send your thoughts to us!
Send to the cloud priests,
Send to the archpriests;
That their songs may bring the waters
To fructify the Earth;
That the Sun embrace the Earth
That she bring forth fruit.

IV

People of the lightning,
Send your serpent darting arrows!
Hear the thunder beating
With its wings of dark cloud!

Who is this that cometh?
People of the trees on the six world mountains,
Standing up to pray for rain,

All your people and your thoughts
    Come to us!

Who is this that cometh?
    People of the dark cloud,
    Let your thoughts come to us!
People of the lightning,
    Let your thoughts come to us!
People of the blue-cloud horizon,
    Let your thoughts come to us!
Rain! Rain! Rain!

Editor's Notes

Published in *Harper's*, June 1921, 79.

"Shipapu" or "Sipapu" is the "mist-encompassed place; underworld of the Pueblos" (Glossary to *Land of Journeys' Ending*); the imagery evokes the Pueblo creation myths, best rendered by Frank Hamilton Cushing, *Zuni Folk Tales* (1901), rpt. New York: Knopf, 1931 and Tucson: University of Arizona Press, 1986.

Songs of the Seasons

I

All these I have mentioned
 With Wawanut;
I have mentioned all the seasons and the stars
 To Wawanut.

All the little steadfast stars
And the Walkers of the Night,
Where the flying light of sun is caught and hidden,
I have named them to Wawanut.

I have named the Thunder,
With his moccasins of dark cloud
Walking on the mountain.
I have named the Tovukmal,
The clean March water
Washing down the last year's leaves.
And the little silver rains,
The many footed rains
Dancing with the meadowlarks
Round the roots of the rainbow.

II

I have named the Pahoyomal
 With Wawanut,
Now the ant has her hill and her house,
The spider opens her door, dew shining;
White butterflies emerging
In their spotted robes
From their sacred dance enclosure.
The wind tosses

The white blossom cones of the chamise,
        And the sea's white foam flowers.

Now the sky is ashamed
Of what he did to the maiden summer;
Retreating afar and on high
He tugs at the four world quarters.

The elk brings forth in the north,
The wild sheep at Temecula,
The horned lizard on the hot sands
Around Turtle Rock
With his young is dancing.

All these I have mentioned in my songs.
I have made a twine of songs
To bind them to Wawanut.

III

I have named the summer
                To Wawanut.
I have mentioned earth's contented noises.
I have named the Star Chief, Kukilish
And the lovely Light-Left-Over-from-the-Evening-to-the-Morning.*

I have named the ripe wild oats
Moon white on the sea-fronting ranges.
Arrows twanging in the white oak browse,
Women stripping deer meat,
All these I have mentioned to Wawanut,
Women winnowing chia.

I have made them songs.
With a net of songs I bind them

To Wawanut.
On the silver-glimmer path
My songs are walking
With Wawanut.

I am proud of my songs,
I have believed my songs.
I have made the seasons and the stars
Work together with Wawanut.

*The planet Venus.

Editor's Notes

In note 15 of *American Rhythm*, Austin calls the poems of this group "rather saturations than re-expressions" because they do not translate "some specific Amerind composition" but use "only Amerind thought." Austin does note that "there is a cycle of Songs of the Season among the Luiseño of Southern California, which concludes with the magic formula of belief as I have closed this, but the rest is largely inferred." The statements are misleading, for the main source for the three poems is Constance Goddard DuBois's full account of Luiseño religious ceremonies and songs. In particular, Austin appears to have used the Luiseño ceremonial songs of the seasons called *Temenganesh*. Indeed, in *AU* 563, Austin notes the influence of DuBois's work, but she drops that point in the published work. Several of the images and phrases in the three poems of "Songs of the Seasons" appear in DuBois, 105–7. Wawanut also appears in Luiseño ceremonies as *Wanawut*, an object of milkweed twine used in boys' puberty ceremony. The ceremony and Wanawut are described in DuBois, 85–87. In both ceremonies, Wanawut symbolizes "the Milky Way, the Spirit to whom our spirits go when they die" (86).

I: "Tovukmal refers to the little streams of water washing the fallen leaves" (DuBois, 165).

II: *Pahoyomal* is the name for early spring, when snakes crawl out, frogs sing, and trees are juicy and ready to put out leaves; DuBois, 107. Chamise is the common flowering shrub *Adenostoma fascicula*, native to California and also called greasewood; Temecula Valley, between Orange County and San Diego, is the site of Pechanga Indian Reservation of Luiseño Indians. DuBois describes the origins of the Temecula people and the significance of the turtle rock landmark, 115, 158–60.

III: *Kukilish* = *Nukulish*, the Luiseño term for the giant red star Antares; DuBois 162; *chia* = *Salvia hispanica*, seeds used for porridge, a staple of Native America.

Prayer to the Mountain Spirit

Young Man, Chieftain,
Reared within the Mountain,
Lord of the Mountain,
Hear a young man's prayer!

Hear a prayer for cleanness
Keeper of the he rain,
Drumming on the mountain,
Lord of the she rain
That restores the earth in newness;
Keeper of the clean rain,
Hear a prayer for wholeness!

Young man, Chieftain,
Hear a prayer for fleetness,
Keeper of the deer's way,
Reared among the eagles,
Clear my feet of slothness!
Keeper of the Paths of Men,
Hear a prayer for straightness!

Hear a prayer for courage!
Keeper of the lightning,
Reared amid the thunder,
Keeper of the dark cloud
At the doorway of the morning,
Hear a prayer for staunchness.

Young man, Chieftain,
Spirit of the Mountain!

Prayer to the Mountain Spirit (From the Navajo)

Lord of the Mountain,
Reared within the Mountain
Young Man, Chieftain,
Hear a young man's prayer!
Hear a prayer for cleanness.
Keeper of the strong rain,
Drumming on the mountain;
Lord of the small rain
That restores the earth in newness;
Keeper of the clean rain,
Hear a prayer for wholeness,

Young Man, Chieftain,
Hear a prayer for fleetness.
Keeper of the deer's way,
Reared among the eagles,
Clear my feet of slothness.
Keeper of the paths of men,
Hear a prayer for straightness.

Hear a prayer for courage.
Lord of the thin peaks,
Reared amid the thunders;
Keeper of the headlands
Holding up the harvest,
Keeper of the strong rocks
Hear a prayer for staunchness.

Young Man, Chieftain,
Spirit of the Mountain!

Editor's Notes

Published in *Poetry*, February 1917, 239; reprinted in *Path on the Rainbow*, 221.

Song of the Mateless Woman

This is my song that I make,
A song for all women
For whom light hands have lit love
A ruining fire in the grasslands,
Strewing its pleasant ways with ash,
And charred sticks of remembrance.

Thus do the mateless women,
Binding their hearts with song,
Lest the gods hear them aching;
Moving on wounded wing
Between their love and the gods,
Lest by the trail of their bleeding hearts
Furies should track the Beloved.

With what cry shall I cry to the gods,
Now my power has departed?

It has gone from me clutching at love,
As the shadow clutching the feet of light
Goes from the mountain.

As the wild geese at the end of rains
Go northward,
As the tang from a wet bow-string,
So is my power gone from me!
How shall I win it again
Who cannot win the love of a man?

With what cry shall I cry,
When my heart is emptied of all
But the grief of women?

All the anguish of women,
It smells to the gods
As the dead after battle.
It sounds in my heart
As the hollow drums,
Calling to battle!

I shall bind up all my pangs
As arrows,
In the sheath of my loneness.
Keen be they as my sorrows!

Return to me, O my Power!
It is I that call,
The Medicine Woman,
Childless, unmated—

Nay, I shall mate with the gods,
And the tribesmen shall be my children!

Rise up in me, O my Power!
As the wings of eagles!
Return on me as the rain,
The earth renewing.
Refresh the springs of my soul
By the path of hidden waters.
Be to me, O my Power,
As the lightning
Out of the fringes of dark cloud
Renewing the harvest.
Make my heart fruitful
To nourish my children.

This is my song that I make,
The song of the mateless woman!

None holdeth my hand
But the Friend-of-the-soul-of-man.

We shall beget great deeds between us!

[And my heart is emptied of all]

And my heart is emptied of all
But the grief of women.

All the anguish of women,
It smells to the gods
As the dead after battle,
It sounds in my heart
As the hollow drums calling to battle,
And the gods come quickly.

Now I shall make a new song,
A song of the grief of women;
But for myself,
But for all who have eaten sorrow,
Who are sick and ashamed
And for love go ahungered—

Come, O my power,
Indwelling spirit!
It is I that call.
Childless, unmated—

Nay, I shall mate with the gods,
And the tribesmen shall be my children.
Rise up in me, O, my power,
On the wings of eagles!
Return upon me as the rain
The earth renewing,
Make my heart fruitful
To nourish my children.

This is my song that I make,
I, the Chisera,

The song of the mateless woman;
None holdeth my hand but the Friend,
In the silence, in the secret places
We shall beget great deeds between us!

Editor's Notes

In act 3 of *The Arrow Maker* (1911), the Chisera comes forward at the judgment of Simwa and makes this speech. Chisera is a witch or medicine woman; see the introduction and Austin's novel *The Flock* (1906), 215–55.

Black Prayers

There is a woman
Has taken my man from me.

How was I to know,
When I gave him my soul to drink
In the moon of Corn Planting,
When the leaves of the oak
Are furred like a mouse's ear,
And the moon curls like a prayer plume
In the green streak over Tyuonyi?

When I poured my soul to his
In the midst of my body's trembling,
How was I to know
That the soul of a woman was no more to him
Than sweet sap dripping
From a bough wind-broken?

If I had known
I could have kept my soul from him,
Even though I kept not my body.

That woman, with her side-looking eyes.
Whatever she takes from him,
It is my soul she is taking.
Waking sharply at night
I can feel my life pulled from me,
Like water in an unbaked olla.
Then I know he is with her,
She is drinking from his lips
The soul I gave him.

Therefore I make black prayers for her
With this raven's feather,
With owl feathers edged with silence,
That all her days may be night-haunted;
Let blackness come upon her,
The downward road
Toward Sipapu;
Let her walk in the shadow of silence.

Would I had kept my soul
Though I gave my body.
Better the sly laugh and the pointed finger
Than this perpetual gnawing of my soul
By a light woman.

Now I know why these witches are so fair,
They are fed on the hearts of better women.
Who would not take another's man,
Knowing there is no untying
The knot of free-given affection.

Let darkness come upon her.
Let her feet stumble
Into the Black Lake of Tears.
Let her soul drown.
Let Those Above not hear her.
By the black raven's plume,
By the owl's feather!

Editor's Notes

Published in *Poetry*, January 1920, 183–85.

Tyuonyi is a large circular pueblo in Frijoles Canyon, northwest of Santa Fe, along the Rio Grande River; it is considered a larger town of the Classic period, 1375–1600, and is now part of Bandelier National Monument.

Olla is an earthenware pot or jar, used for cooking or storing water.

Sipapu is the place of emergence of the Pueblos; see Austin, *Land of Journeys' Ending*, 416, and glossary.

Songs in the American Manner

A Preface for a Book

This is the house of my heart.
The unlatched casement
Swings to the street
And clacks to the wind's advertisement.
Wanton the house is become
To the eyes of the neighbors.

Rare are the rooms within.
The windows
Look on the wood and the sea
And the lifting surf, seven-colored.
Sweet are the airs of the house,
Mixed of the sea and the sun-steeped roses;
Sweet and secret the halls
And morning haunted the chambers.

But ever the Lord of the house
Lingers abroad and afar;
And ever the unlatched casement
And the door aswing on its hinges,
Let in the envious stranger,
Desiring the pictured walls
And the seaward-looking windows.
Ever the lit hearth leaps

And the shadow fire in the twilight
Beckon the Lord of the house
With the ache of an empty dwelling.

Would he might come to his house
And shut up the clacking casement!

Song of the Maverick

I am too arid for tears, and for laughter
Too sore with unslaked desires.
My nights are scanty of sleep
And my sleep too full of dreaming;
The frosts are not cold enough
Nor the suns sufficiently burning:
The hollow waves are slack
And no wind from any quarter
Lifts strongly enough to outwear me.
My body is bitter with baffled lusts
Of work and love and endurance.
As a maverick, leaderless, lost from the herd,
Loweth my soul with the need of man encounters.

For I am crammed and replete
With the power of desolate places;
I have gone far on faint trails
And slept in the shade of my arrows;
Paticncc, forgiveness and might
Ache in me, finding no egress,
And virtues stale that are too big for the out gate.

I would run large with the man herd, the hill subduers,
I would impress myself on the mold of large adventure
Until all deeds of that likeness
Should a long time carry
The stripe of the firstling's father.

For I am anguished with strength,
Overfed with the common experience,
My feet run wide of the rutted trails
Toward the undared destinies.

Editor's Notes

First published in Austin's nonfiction book, *Christ in Italy* (1912).

The Much Desired

I have heard a voice awake in the dawn dim valleys,
A shout from the rearing hills hand-fasted under the headlands,
Where the wild sheep are,
And the trails are hid by the heather;
Whose hands are under the earth for the travail of the harvests.
For I have lain on the hills and the strong wind hath covered me,
I have seen the Much Desired, white as wheat in September.

You that hark for the sea in a shell, hollow and pearled and
precious,
He is here by the surf that rings the brown foreshore with thunder!
He has left the dropping shrines for the altar lift of the mesas!
Far are His feet in the dew from the man infested places.

Not in the old, old house whose props were flawed in the casting;
Not with the old, old sword, crumpled and dulled at the edges!
Strained little souls that creep to bedizened, ancient altars,
I heard Him pass in the wind
The sea blue lilacs bent under;
Who knows but for you He will stop and cover your lack with His
garments!

Who cares whither the King has gone, whom He has blessed in
parting?
I have seen wings astir that left the heavens tender,
And I am hushed with happiness
And I am dumb with wonder,
You shall know me where I go by the smell of the meadows,
The scent of the broken scrub and the yerba buena,
I have been breaking trail for the Much Desired!

Editor's Notes

Yerba buena are any of several aromatic species of mint, applied by early Spanish missionaries in California; it is also an early name for San Francisco.

First published in Austin's nonfiction book, *Christ in Italy* (1912).

You That Go by in the Street

Sisters, my sisters,
You that go by in the street,
Seeking the starry adventure,
Is it the hour or the man,
Is it love you seek or the lover?

Flithering moths of the bright barred night,
Scarred at Love's mighty candle,
Strange I should know so well
What the lit street provides you!
Snatched from the gulf for an hour
By a dear bought preciousness,
Turning your cheek on a transient breast
For the ease of an aching remembrance.

Sisters, my sisters.
Between my bed and the wall,
In the void of my aching,
I am aware of a winding stair
Love by light love leading down,
Each one lighter than each
To the guttered slime of the roadway.
That way great Love went down,
After the use of the street,
Not looking backward.
Sisters, my sisters,
The mark of the street between my breasts,
Will it grow white with weeping?

Unworthy Love

How is it with my heart
Since I can love thee?
Flawed in the casting,
So that thy soul
When I strike it with nobleness
Rings no tone truly.

Yet, at that flattened note
The soul of every sense
Shouldering each on each
Runs and looks out of the windows
While deep in the house of Life
Age-long, unimagined instincts
Bay at the voice of the master.

Editor's Notes

Published in *Poetry*, January 1921, 192.

Woman

When woman lay in the womb of the world,
Ere the heart of the world was divided,
Before there was faith or forsaking,
They heard what the high gods said,
Making, unmaking.

Heard it small and apart, as a spider
Dropped from her gossamer thread
Heareth far overhead
The talk of the forest.

Darkly as pines that confer,
Their high tops bowed together
In the Wills that blow between the worlds,
Fingering the Wills for the thread that binds
The upper world and the nether;—
The will of each to each in its kind,
And the will of all to Oneness.

"Lo," said the makers of men,
Ere man was molded,
Sitting under the Wills as in dreams men should see them
Shaping our eldern earth under an Ash tree,
"Sow we the Word unto Life as the linden
Scatters her summer winged seeds to the windy spaces,
Even so as it falls, we shall take counsel together
For the sake of man that we make, lest the Wills rend him
Eyeless, untiring, rotting, reforming—
Binding him fast unto Life, we shall fend him
With the will of each unto each in his kind,
And the will of all to Oneness."

Then the Word went glinting forth,
As between the sun and the dawning
The silken fleets of the milkweed
Sail in the windless air above the marshes;
In the days when the Man within man
Stood up from the Beast his brother.
And suddenly Life was stirred.
As the prows in the harbor
Move all at once and together
When the land wind begins,
And deeper than surf or tide
The sea dreams of adventure.

Up leaped the doe from the fern
When the buck belled her,
Leaving the uncropped scrub and the bindweed blossom,
Following nose on flank, dappled and antlered;
Afar at her killing, the Voice of the lonely land
Answered the roar of her lord in the hot blue dawning;
Mellowly out of his thicket whistled the hermit thrush,
And "True true true" moaned the doves by the water courses.

Small and afar, as a spider climbs to the sun,
The woman climbed up to life by the thread from her body spun,
And she marked through the leaf and bloom of life
How the changing patterns run
In the Wills that blow across the world
As the wind across the wheat,
And the opal bubbles of love frothed up
And broke in slime at her feet.
But she braved the rending forces,
And she dared the Wills to meet,
For the Word was in her bosom,
Ere ever life begun,

*

The will of each to each in its kind
And the will of us all to One.

Editor's Notes

First published in Austin's nonfiction book, *Love and the Soul Maker* (1914), under the title "Word That Came to Women."

The Wound That Bled in Heaven

There was a man of Nazareth
Whose wounds ached in Heaven.
Under the tree whose leaves
Floating from noon to noon of the centuries
Marked out a day of the Lord,
Where the Seraphim
Dipped their bright wings in the river,
Lo, in his pierced hands,
He was aware of a pang,
And the track of a spear in his side
Reddened and throbbing.

Straightway forth from the gate
He followed the ache in his breast, as a homing pigeon
Follows the secret clue to the cote that bred him;
Marked by none but the angels
Tossing their moon bright spheres in the windless spaces,
Leaving them poised in the void while they wondered,
Touched with awe of his manhood,
With a faint celestial envy
Of his strange, great gift of sorrow
And the wound that bled in Heaven.

Not at all men marked him
As he went in his earlier guise of a race rejected,
With sweated brows
And palms that the adze had calloused.
But for all their common stripe,
It was not the Workers stayed him.

In the cry of yoke-galled people,
Said the man of Nazareth,
There is nothing new or strange to set my side bleeding.

It is not my yoke that they bear, nor my burden.
It was neither blood nor sweat that bowed me,
But the burden of strength
And the yoke of rebellion.
I was not all for pity, even on earth,
Said the man of Nazareth.

Loud in Heaven, he said to his own,
In the rent paid pews where he found them,
Is the cry of the young, defrauded
Of the beast's right to the sun
And the well fed stature.
The tears of soul blind children
Scald the wound in my side,
Said the man of Nazareth.
Lord, said his own, with a fine Christian courtesy,—
Noting the marks of his trade with eyes averted,—
In the building of States
There must needs be some tools broken,
Children put too soon to the wheel,
In the rash way of the poor.
Lord, you have seen it,
When of your great condescension
You came to the scum of the earth
From your high, exclusive Heaven.
The poor have not greatly changed, O Lord,
Since you knew them.

Yea, said the man of Nazareth.
It is for this my wounds bleed
Even in Heaven.

Editor's Notes

Published in *Harper's Weekly*, May 23, 1914, 15.

Whence?

I do not know who sings my songs
Before they are sung by me.

For my mind is an ordered house
Where never a song should be;
And the world is the sort of a place
That my inquiring spirit grieves.
Yet when my thoughts are seated round
With their eyes upon the ground,
The little songs come flimmering
Like swallows round the eaves.

And when my life is as dry as a gourd,
My heart the pebble, rattled by despair,
Shaken at the funeral
Of all the gods that were,
I stretch my thoughts in the empty room—
And suddenly my songs are there.

Editor's Notes

Published in *Poetry*, January 1921, 192.

Young Love Remembered

Young, oh, young!
And yet stronger than the years.
There was never breast but yours
That could prop the ache in mine,
Save the hollow of your shoulder
Is no comfort for my tears.
Strange that love so short and hurried
For so long should wake and cry,
And the dreams come back unburied,
For not one of them will die.

Ebia, Mother of Men

Ebia, mother of men.
From the door of her cave delivering judgment.

Say unto man, my son, that he wakes me;
I that have slumbered so long in the breasts of all women.
Now is my dreaming pierced with the noise of his beast-hood,
Spitting his teeth through the long black tubes
Into his brother's vitals;
Where with the steel forged hand he rendeth his fellows
Till the slayer lies down on the slain
In the red wallows.

Thus of old in their rages
Drummed the great males on their breasts in the dew-chilled
    dawning
When sick with fear of the beast, I put the beast habit from off me;
Clasping my son in my arms
Through the forest I fled uprightly.
Yea, I am shaken in sleep with the ancient terrors
Or ever the tribes were named or the man-thought fashioned,
When the hand that he clasped in mine
As the viewless fear pursued us
Was the first that he took from the ground,
Learning to go uprightly.

Soft have I slumbered here in the breasts of women,
Under the summer-shed bloom of womanly graces,
Virtues thick on my head as the leaves of the forest,
Feeding the fruit of the race in the sky-spread branches.
Say unto man, my son, have a care how he wakes me;
Lest I arise again in the breasts of all women,
Lest I take my son by the hand
And teach him to go uprightly.

Editor's Notes

Published under the title "War" on the inside cover of *Harper's Weekly*, May 8, 1915.

Fifth Avenue at Night

Long undulating lines of light
Picked at like harpstrings
By the steel-fingered rain.
Slivers of steel,
White sparks of steel struck off
By impact with the pavement,
Glancing *plop*!
Into mirror surfaced pools,
Thin, black puddles of steel
Damascened with gold of glinting lights.

High on either side
Many-windowed facades,
Honeycombed with light.
Half drained of honey
By the rain-sleeked swarms of umbrellas
Darting to cover in subterranean passages,
Leaving the honeyed windows gaping blank
At slithering lines of automobiles,
Black beetle shining,
Each with its one red light
Like the red heart of hurry.

The rain-disheveled lamps
Squatter past the cathedral,
Down Murray Hill
They troop blinking,
To see what the busses are about
Under the arch there,
At the foot of the avenue.

Grasshopper-green busses
Peering at one another

With great goggle lamps of eyes;
Circling and twittering with their heads together,
Scurrying north on inexplicable errands,
Stopping and starting convulsively
Pricked by slivers of rain.

The myriad-windowed facades
Relax behind their veils of rain.
The tension of their angles is loosened by the darkness,
Between flickers of the light they yawn
Like dowagers in the dark intervals of Opera
Dropping their wattles above necklaces of light,
While the orchestral rain tightens its strings
And tunes them to the wind.

Behind them all the high-piled plunder,
The inchoate magpie hordes
Of Tiffany and Magobgob
Are visiting one another.
Egyptian trinkets torn from Pharaoh's tombs
Are exchanging reminiscences
With tinsel from DeBrosses Street.

Editor's Notes

Murray Hill is a neighborhood in midtown Manhattan; Tiffany's flagship store is at 57th Street and Fifth Avenue; DeBrosses Street is in lower Manhattan, near the Holland Tunnel. The name Magobgob recalls the land of Gog and Magog in the Bible and may be of Amharic origin.

I Do Not Know

I do not know if there is God,
The center of this whirling orb
Making and unmaking.

I do not know if there is God—
But there's a Spirit in the wood.

That was it where once the lupine stirred.
And there it laughed
Between two gurgles of the brook and made
Warm silence and the windless stir
Along my sides where once was fur,
And nameless, fierce temptations in my blood.

Or when the dawn is like a trumpet laid
To the sea's lips that are curved keen for it,
When the wet beach is gleaming like a shell,
And all the foreshore whispers in green fire,
I have felt that Spirit pass,
Stalking the young winds in the grass.

I do not know if there is God—

But when my travail came
And every sense went weltering blind
'Round jagged rocks of pain,
There was a swimmer in the surf
Rode with us down the staggering gulf
And brought us safe to land.

. . . The hurrying hearse whisked out of sight,
The sexton cleaned his spade on the grass,
(My grief was stiff like the slithering clay)

And the mourners put up their veils. . . .
There was a Spirit blew
The graveyard dust in my face.

"Earth unto earth was said of you.
For something of you has gone into the ground
With the child that you made at your body's cost.
And a sea-blue lilac cannot toss,
Nor the white corn tassel, row on row,
But something of you has entered there.
The brown corn silk is the brown of her hair,
And the pink of her mouth you will find again
Delicately folded lip on lip, in the budding tips
Of the apricot boughs.
For nothing can ever divide you now
From the earth you have made with your dead."

That was a thing
Only a Spirit could have said.

Editor's Notes

Published in *Poetry*, January 1920, 186–87.

New Mexican Love Song

The long last lights on the mesas fail,
And the coo doves cease,
And the twittering quail
The young wind walks in the tasseling corn
Ohè!

But there's never the fall of your foot in the trail
And the twilight hour is long,
Beloved,
Ohè!
The twilight hour is long!

The moon comes over the cañon wall
The *tombes* wake,
And the slim flutes call,
And the dew drips down the tasseling corn,
Ohè!

But there's never the sound of your voice at all
And the twilight hour is long,
Beloved,
Ohè!
The twilight hour is long!

Editor's Notes

Published in *Poetry*, January 1920, 185–86.

Tombes are ceremonial drums.

Dream

You should have weighted my dream of you
With a leaden reality,
Then it would have gone down
Like some shotted mariner
Stark in his canvas,
Leaving the following seas
All open to the stars!

Being only a dream,
There's never a wave
Lifting from blue to chrysoprase,
Never an opal shine on the wet beaches,
Nor auklet shattering
The twilight's pure obsidian,
Never a swift wing flash of beauty anywhere
But my dream of you is there.

Editor's Notes

Published in *Poetry*, April 1923, 19.

Chrysoprase is the ancient name of a golden-green precious stone (*Oxford English Dictionary*).

On Hearing Vachel Lindsay Chant his Verse

I have remembered whence I came. . . .

Sleek, silt-charged rivers,
Fat loam, slow yielding to the share,
Slithering yellow clay,
Tenacious as the heavy farmer stuff
Cold on the withers of your stallion fancy, Lindsay.

I remember the lush bottoms,
The basson blare of the trumpet creepers,
The glassy air
Shattered by insect glitter.
Slow-moving summer creeks
Laced in light rings
By obscene water moccasins;
And straight as a wound bleeding inwardly,
The red streak of the cardinal.

I remember the towns,
Slab-sided, smug,
Impounding Pegasus among the cockleburs;
The slab-sided men, my forebears,
Bearded like prophets,
But setting a clean-shaven upper lip
Against prophesying in the name of any God but theirs.

Songs I remember. . . .
"Tenting To-night," and "Nicodemus"
Haunting my childhood like gray gulls
Blown inland from deep-sea commotion,
Sung by deep-breasted women,
Large-armed for the cradling of States.
And like a child's dream of a star,

High on a heaven-whitened hill
Old John Brown and his seven sons
Making with God a majority.

Witchfires, outside the window, in the cold twilight,
The beckoning dance, fragmentary, of Old-World Wonder,
And that dim shouter in the offing of my mind,
(You, Lindsay, on your stallion fancy?)

All these I have remembered,
As a man wearing the king's tinsel,
Suddenly sees in the throng gathered to celebrate him,
Strong peasant faces,
Knowing, at once and past any shaming,
How he has climbed by their sinews,
Throws his cockade to the king's lackeys, and declares
There, there alone, are my kinsmen!

Editor's Notes

Vachel Lindsay (1879-1931) was well-known as the "Prairie Troubadour," taking several walking tours across the Midwest and Southwest, supporting himself by reciting his poems. Along with Edgar Lee Masters and Carl Sandburg, he brought the themes of Illinois to the American reader. "Tenting Tonight" and "Wake Nicodemus" were popular songs during the Civil War. John Brown was a dedicated abolitionist who led the famous raid on Harper's Ferry Armory in October 1859; his action and eventual execution contributed to the outbreak of the Civil War.

Going West

Some day I shall go West,
Having won all time to love it in, at last
Too still to boast.

But when I smell the sage,
When the long, marching landscape line
Melts into wreathing mountains,
And the dust cones dance,
Something in me that is of them will stir.

Happy if I come home
When the musk-scented, moon-white gilia blows,
When all the hills are blue, remembering
The sea from which they rose.
Happy again,
When blunt-faced bees carouse
In the red flagons of the incense shrub,
Or apricots have lacquered boughs,
And trails are dim with rain!

Lay me where some contented oak can prove
How much of me is nurture for a tree;
Sage thought of mine
Be acorn clusters for the deer to browse.
My loving whimsies—will you chide again
When they come up as lantern flowers?

I shall be small and happy as the grass,
Proud if my tip
Stays the white, webby moons the spider weaves,
Or down my bleaching stalks shall slip
The light, imprisoning dew.

Where once you trod,
I shall be bluets in the April sod.

Or if the wheel should turn too fast,
Run up and rest
As a sequoia for a thousand years!

Editor's Notes

Published in *Bookman*, September 1922, 8.

Clinging Vines

WOODBINE

He was a tree whose winged seeds
Should have reforested our barren acres;
She was the vine that found him.

Lovelily she bound
Boughs that the four wind-rivers shaped.
That's a vine's nature!
It was our folly praised
Her banners bright against the frost
On tips whose deep, root-driven sap
Made all his seasons spring.

Woodbine was meant to mask hewn rafters
With leafage of reward.
He was a tree. . . .
Earth's immemorial flourish to the light.

Oh, she knew his worth!
Her love was like a flag,
Love red, to show how high he stood
Against the sky and sun,
Wreathed, celebrated;
At last no sun could reach him.
There he stands!
Heart rotted in her clasp.

And still, she has her pride.
All that flame-colored autumn show,
That's her fine loyalty,
Never to let us know
'Tis she that keeps him standing.

WILD CUCUMBER

Here on our lower mesa there's a vine
Called megharizza,
Comes from a strong, man-shaped root.

The first of our Spring rains
Brings its translucent, pulsing shoots
All silvery pubescent,
Like lad's love,
Every tip alert
As to the glance of some bright girl.

Warm, growing days they move
Clockwise to slightest intimations of support,
Your body, or the nearest cañon wall,
That fish-hook cactus,
Taken with the happy confidence
Of an unchidden child.

She was like that!
No matter what she leaned on
She had some tendrils feeling toward the sun.
If in you she found
Vantage for her next reach,
You were by so much honored.

Women never understood her!
Women think loving must have consequences.
Children, or, at least
Serve as the overture
To notable achievement.
Love was the mode of her existence.

'Tis true she grew . . . exuberant.

*

Those coarsely yellowing leaves
Strung from the splay-footed oak,
That papery, prickling pod
You rattled with your foot . . .
Wild Cucumber, not fit for food!

Still, I think the oak was happier
For those pale green, star-pointed panicles;
They smell of earth, you notice,
Moist earth on the first nights of Spring,
And the strong, man-shaped root. . . .
But women seldom understand!

Fig Leaves

The poet Sterling once
Said of a mayfly book,
Glinting across the wind-sown field of print,
"It has no guts."
And with male squeamishness, apologized,
Not knowing
That women who have felt beneath their breath
The announcing drumbeat of a life beginning,
Have not man's need of fig-leaf phrases.

At any rate he needn't have apologized to me
Who had seen the Red Man dancing
To sustain the World Throb penned
Alive between his ribs,
Not like a ballerina's, in her toes,
But next to where his life is;
Heart, breath and bowels of him, moved
With the desire to make the world work well with God,
Or the proud consciousness
Of having made a woman know him for a man,
Till the laced muscles eased him into sound,
And all his thought, filmed into words,
Rose like linked bubbles in a rain-fed spring,
And song became
A symbol that fulfilled itself.

No guts. . . .

Perhaps that's why we have no poets now
Can grip the people with creative pain;
But star cold music such as Sterling makes,
Or the free versifier's choice, eviscerated phrases,
Or braying of maimed voices,

Hybrids of art and sociology,
Blaming the world and us for their lost potency.
Dante and Homer and Isaiah came
When the effective motions of man's mind,
Courage, remorse, compassion,
Lived each in its vital organ,
Where the Kingdom of God is, in the midst of us.
What else is music but the pang,—
Wrung from the entrails of some poor, dead beastie,—
By which the outgoing sense of things
Catches you in the midriff?

God, when He first began to make Him creatures,
Fashioned them of guts.
A little pulse, a little pouch for food,
A film between them and the Universe.
Brain, motion, and the serviceable hand,
So many figures of the dance
Of the red-gutted microcosms,
Throbbing to rhythms long rehearsed,—
The soul—a song our viscera makes to God.

Editor's Notes

The poet George Sterling (1869-1926) was one of Austin's close friends during her years in Carmel, California. See "Three at Carmel" in Magazine and Periodical Publications.

Women's War Thoughts

A room in Time from which a window looks on the Present.

THE TRUMPETS:

Wake, O Women!

A WOMAN AT THE WINDOW:

Oh, no more for women
Shall the trumpets tear their throats!

No more the white riders,
Strong thewed and breastless
Come reiving and raiding.
We modern women
Are undone by our own preciousness.
Like viols of few strings
Plucked at by lovers in their silken intervals,
Live in the prelude to our womanness.
Our music seldom swings
From the appassionata's opening phrases
Into the star-built theme of mastery.

Not even like the Spartan women,
Guardians of the Gate whereby life, entering, is made man
By virtue of that clean divinity
That lives in women's flesh.
Not ours to turn,
Whose sons return not
Borne on their shields or bearing them,
To rear a sterner offspring to our conquerors.

Trumpets sound, and summoning drums.

Our sons are too much ours!

Too much the child, that means,
Too prone to keep us
The condoning lap, the leaned on bosom,
The ever pleased spectator of their plays
Filling the gaps with ready make believe.

We talk of giving,
Who cannot throb to world adventure
Save through the still unsevered stalk of being;
Who suffer, deep in the womb of our affection,
Perpetual pangs of parturition.

Suddenly the drums
Quicken the male pulse of the world,
The questing trumpets
Seek out the part of them that is not us,
And with a sword
Time heals us of a too prolonged maternity.

Flags go by, and the tips of bayonets, passing the window in full procession.

Strange they should look so much alike!

I cannot find my son's
Among the lean brown shanks,
Crossing and uncrossing like the shears of Atropos
To cut the thread of over-ripe autocracy.
Nor trace the alien strains
Gave rise to that steel-glinting river,
Frothed bright with banners.

What tongues do trumpets speak,
Welding all men into one moving unit?

Women are welded at heart
By the rhythm of rocking cradles.

World-wide, they are starting awake to feel if one is well covered,
Who at that moment may be lying stark in the trenches.
Women of any nation,
For the sake of a long sheared curl
Between two leaves of a prayer book,
Will weep on each other's shoulders.

But the word of the trumpet to men
Is the seed of a forthright intention.
The drums go by, and the Allied banners.
When I was young, my son,
I dreamed of a life exempted as yours is to-day,
From the claims of the past and the present,
A tiny, two-penny candle to burn on the altar of Now.

But the cant of a world made sleek by soul-stroking phrases,
Offered your life for mine.
As though your life were a thing I could make
For my soul's diversion,
To dangle before my mind
And quiet its hunger.
Oh, my son, how times like these give the lie
To that smug maternal illusion!

VOICES OF YOUNG SOLDIERS (*singing*):

Land, my Land!
Thy sons are going
Where like a wind from the west we feel God blowing
Kings from their seats and Empire from its stays.
Land where the Vision blessed our fathers,
Perfect in us thy praise!

THE WOMAN (*repeating the word of the inner Voice*):

. . . You are no more to the making
Than the nozzle is to the fountain.
I am the source and the stream
And the deeps to which I have called him.
I will drink up the life of your son
To quicken my harvest.
I will take up his life and lay it
To the lips of my larger purpose,
Trumpeting forth my power,
And my will to Freedom . . .

YOUNG SOLDIERS (*singing*):

Land, my Land!
Thy sons go singing
Forth to the work of our God, our lives free flinging
Nothing withholden or scamped, for thy sake;
Land, by whose voice the larger Freedom
Has called the world awake!

THE WOMAN (*muses*):

Life that passed through us,
Did it leave no tang of the man strain, mordant, unruly . . .
The Red Cross nurses go by.
Yonder the barren women . . .
Women whose breasts are scarcely grown
But whose hearts are steadied with skill,
Will sit on the Pit's red edge
And hold back death with laughter.

Bite back the moan in your throat, O my son,
If the shrapnel tears you.
Lest the unwed women say
I was too woman-soft when I shaped you,

I that am left to hand-waving, balcony service!

The music grows faint in the distance.

Why should we weep
Who taught them to follow the music;
We who attuned them
To feints, pursuits, and surprises?
Have we ever denied them the game that we should wonder
When they go roaring forth to hunt one another?

Blood . . .

There is no virtue in blood . . .
Any woman will tell you!

Torn flesh . . . and a gay endurance . . .
I did as much for you in the bearing.

War is a sickness sucked from your shiny, toy maleness.
When your teeth have met on hard metal awhile
You will be cured of your sickness.

And then, . . .
We will go back to our playing,
Sally, retreat, and ambush, handling and stroking,
Till Peace is choked with the rising scum
Of our passionate prepossessions.

Was it you or I, son,
Made this war, I wonder!

Editor's Notes

Published in *Dial*, November 1921, 551–55.

The American Rhythm, 1930

In the 1930 edition of *The American Rhythm*, Austin deleted six poems from the "Amerindian Songs" section and added fifteen new "re-expressions" to make a total of forty-two "Amerindian Songs." She also added two new sections to the book: "Magic Formulas from the Cherokee" and "Tribal Lays." These new sections are "re-expressions," too, closely aligned with sources in the publications of the American Bureau of Ethnology, harking back to the work of earlier ethnologists such as James Mooney, Pliny Earle Goddard, Frank Hamilton Cushing, and Francis La Flesche. She added a number of explanatory footnotes, and she could claim in *Earth Horizon* that the new edition of *The American Rhythm* was "a complete edition" and that "now there is no American anthology that does not quote it, and few Western poets who do not filch from it. Even Amy Lowell did that, but she had the grace to blush when I referred to it" (345). All of Austin's original poems in the "Songs in the American Manner" section were deleted. Thus Austin seems to have considered the 1930 edition of *The American Rhythm* an anthology of Native American poems, not as a collection of her own poetry.

In the new edition of *The American Rhythm*, Austin provided some eighteen pages of "Addenda" for the introduction. In the first addendum to the 1930 introduction, Austin updates her list of modern heirs to American landscape and Amerindian song, focusing on the role of abstraction in dance, visual and plastic arts, and poetry. She particularly notes the poetry of T. S. Eliot, E. E. Cummings, Ezra Pound, D. H. Lawrence, and Robinson Jeffers in relation to abstract expression, and, as in the 1923 edition, she praises Sandburg, Frost, and Lindsay for the "growing conformity" of their work to their specific landscapes (*AR* 67). Many readers today will find this 1930 list more predictably modernist than Austin's 1923 lists. In the first third of the twentieth century, however, and particularly in the years surrounding World War I, Masters, Lindsay, and Sandburg—Midwesterners all—were strongly associated with a new, democratic poetry that evoked the common life of American farmers and laborers. Frost was especially innovative in his vigorous colloquial language. Lawrence had moved to Taos, New Mexico, in 1922, writing his *Studies in Classic American Literature* during the two years he stayed there, so he was a personal acquaintance of Austin. For most of these writers, the free-verse form of their major work firmly placed them in the tradition of Whitman and marked them as writing avant-garde poetry. Meanwhile, the major works of high modernists like Pound, Eliot, and Cummings appeared after the first edition of *The American Rhythm* was published, while Robinson Jeffers's characteristic poetry of California dates from the late 1920s and after. David Perkins discusses these poets in his excellent history of modern American and English poetry, *A History of Modern Poetry: From the 1890s to the High Modernist Mode* (Cambridge: Belknap, 1976).

The second addendum to the 1930 edition is Austin's increased emphasis on the magic power of Amerindian songs. She had already written on the subject in the introduction to *Path on the Rainbow*, and the topic looms large in the early essay, "The Song Makers," from 1911. In "The Song Makers," Austin dramatizes an evening of conversation with Kern River Jim and Tinnemaha, a medicine man of the Owens Valley Paiute tribe. Tinnemaha teaches Austin the role of dance in the ceremonial songs of the Paiute: "'We dance always,' said he. 'It is the shortest road to the Friend of the Soul of Man'" (*MASW*, 256). Eventually Austin states her epiphany:

> Good Medicine! There I had the whole business of songmakers; painted songs, printed songs, or whatever; not to preach, not to please merely, but to make a short road to the mood of power, to touch the Friend. But you had by Tinnemaha's account to touch him yourself first, to swing up by the skirts of the Great Moment and to let down a hand to stumbling men. (*MASW*, 258)

Tinnemaha makes an important appearance in the 1930 edition of *The American Rhythm*, reciting for Austin the cycle of twin brother tales, the last of which she reproduces in a prose translation (*AR*, 143–46). Austin describes the performance in detail, even though she admits that it was "early in this study" of Amerindian art, and she evokes a combination of narrative and music: "There was music; not a song. It had no words nor any tune. It had time, which was clicked out by the singing elders with willow wands, in one end of which a wedge-shaped split had been made for a matter of a foot or two. Properly handled, they produced a sound like the smooth continuous rattle of castanets, but softer, and beautifully synchronized. To this accompaniment the music wandered, a thread of unpatterned melody, unpatterned as blowing wind or flowing water" (*AR*, 78). The description is itself magical in its evocation of the performance, and Austin uses her trademark landscape imagery to suggest the magic power of Amerindian art. But Austin ends the description with ironic humor: "A singular and engaging instance; too singular to prove anything!" (79). As the 1930 introduction draws to a close, Austin continually suggests enormous opportunities for more work in collecting, understanding, and translating Amerindian narratives, myths, and epics. The additional poems and prose texts in the 1930 edition of *The American Rhythm* support the emphasis that Austin gives to magic power and diverse poetic forms in the expanded introduction.

Amerindian Songs Re-expressed from the Originals

A Song of Greatness

When I hear the old men,
Telling of heroes,
Telling of great deeds of ancient days,
When I hear that telling,
Then I think within me
I, too, am one of these.

When I hear the tribesmen
Praising great ones,
Praising warriors of ancient days,
When I hear that praising
Then I know that I, too,
Shall be esteemed,
I, too, when my time comes,
Shall do mightily.

Sioux?

Editor's Notes

Note 16: Austin says she got the song from a Sioux boy, but he wasn't sure of its origin, and song borrowing is frequent.

Personal Song of Red Fox

On that stone ridge I go,
Hauh, hauh!
East I go,
Hauh, hauh!
On the white road I go
Crouching I go,
Hauh, hauh!
I yelp on the road of stars.
Hauh, hauh.

Northern California.

Editor's Notes

Reprinted from *The Children Sing in the Far West*.

Song of a Woman Abandoned by the Tribe Because she is too Old to Keep up with their Migration

Alas, that I should die,
That I should die now,
I who know so much!

It will miss me,
The twirling fire stick;
The fire coal between the hearth stones,
It will miss me.

The Medicine songs,
The songs of magic healing;
The medicine herbs by the water borders,
They will miss me;
The basket willow,
It will miss me;
All the wisdom of women,
It will miss me.

Alas, that I should die,
Who know so much.

Southern Shoshone.

Personal Song of Daniel Red Eagle

The fierce hawk of death is over me,
The fierce hawk of death.

Now and again
Its wing shadows
Brush my shoulders.

The fierce hawk of death,
When will it strike!

Oglalla Sioux.

Song of Seeking

The dear of my soul
I have lost it;
That lost Other
I am seeking;
All night awake
I am seeking.
I shall leave no place unsearched till I find her.
At day break,
I seemed to see her,
It was only
The flash of a loon's wing on the water,
It is not that Other whom my soul seeketh.

Chippewa.

Thunder Dance at San Ildefonso

I

We are calling on the dark cloud
Calling on the dun cloud,
On the eagle-feathered clouds
From their mountain eyries.
Come, clouds, come
And bring the summer rain.

II

Hear the thunder calling
With the voice of many villages,
With the sound of hollow drums,
With the roll of pebbled gourds
Like the swish of rushing rain.
Hoonah, hoonah,
The voice of the thunder
Calling on the clouds to bring the summer rain.

III

Slow   cloud
Low   cloud
Wing-hovering cloud
Over the thirsty fields,
Over the waiting towns
Low   cloud, slow   cloud
Let the rain down!

Over the blossoming beans
Over the tasseling corn.

All day over the thirsty fields
Let the rain down!

Tewa.

Editor's Notes

The San Ildefonso pueblo is one of six pueblos north of Santa Fe, New Mexico, that are associated with the Tewa culture and language. As Elsie Parsons notes, "Probably no Pueblo ceremony is without song or prayer for moisture" (*Pueblo Indian Religion* I: 481). See "Song of the Basket Dancers" in *AR*, 1923.

Cradle Song

Coo . . . ah . . . coo . . . !
Little Dove,
Coo . . ah . . coo!

The wind is rocking
Thy nest in the pine bough,
My arms are rocking
Thy nest, little Dove.

Coo . . . ah. . . . coo
Little Dove
Sleep Little Dove
Coo . . oo . oooo Little Dove!

Paiute.

Gambling Song

OFTEN SUNG AS A LULLABY

Glossy Locks picks them up,
Picks them up, picks them up.

Red Moccasin picks them up,
Picks them up,
The Winning ones,
The Lucky ones,
Glossy Locks picks them up
My little Dove!

Navajo.

Editor's Notes

Austin's source for the lullabies and gambling songs is Washington Matthews, "Navajo Gambling Songs," *American Anthropologist* 2 (January 1889): 1–19; rpt. Washington, D.C.: Judd & Detweiler, 1889; a similar gambling poem appears in *The Children Sing in the Far West* as "Glossy Locks."

Two Songs of Victory

COMMEMORATIVE SONG AND DANCE OF PAIUTES FOR A VICTORY OVER THE MOJAVE

Hey-yah, hey-yah, hey
Ha . aha . ha-ha

(The dancers circle the fire holding bows in position for stooping shots.)

This is what we do,
This is what we do,
This is what we do to our enemies.

(They leap, as over dead bodies stretched on the ground.)

Hah!
The feast is spread,
Come to the feast,
O ye vultures,
On wide wings soaring,
Come to the feast,
O ye vultures!

(Dancers balance their arms like wings, and leap over the swelling bodies.)

Hey-yah, hey-yah, hey,
Ha, aha, ha-ha,
This is the feast we have spread.

VICTORY SONG OF THE FOX

I

I am the one that was blessed,
I am the one.
The sharp arrows of our enemies,
From me they turned aside.
I am the one whose body
Was made holy.

II

They begin to whet their beaks,
Those sacred ones,
Those hungry ones.
They whet their forked beaks
They begin to open their mouths
In the middle of the sky,
Those hungry ones.
They move their beaks, assembling.

Song of a Man Whose Father was Killed in War

Something red my father wears now,
Where his life was.

O young men,
Whose wound stripes are on your sleeves
Walk you reverently
Pronouncing my father's name.

O my father,
I hear the old men saying
There goes a warrior's son.

Sioux.

Editor's Notes

Reprinted from *The Children Sing in the Far West*.

Song of a Man About to Die in a Strange Land

If I die here
In a strange land,
If I die
In a land not my own,
Nevertheless, the thunder
The rolling thunder
Will take me home.

If I die here, the wind,
The wind rushing over the prairie,
The wind will take me home.

The wind and the thunder,
They are the same everywhere,
What does it matter, then,
If I die here in a strange land?

Ojibway.

Editor's Notes

Reprinted from *The Children Sing in the Far West.*

Pilgrimage Song

WOMAN'S DANCE AT TESUQUE PUEBLO

That mountain there,
That white-shell mountain,
Toward the east it standeth,
O sacred mountain,
Whence the day springs.
O white-shell mountain,
Guard thou our day!

Yonder, afar,
That dark blue mountain,
Toward the north standing
That sacred mountain,
Whence the storm cometh,
O dark blue mountain,
Spare not our storm!

That mountain there,
That turquoise-colored mountain,
Toward the west it standeth,
The path of life unending
And beyond it,
O turquoise mountain,
Guide thou our way!

Yonder, afar,
Rose-yellow mountain,
Sacred southern mountain,
Yonder afar, in beauty walking,
The way of joy unending;
Rose-yellow mountain,
Keep thou our home!

Editor's Notes

The Tesuque Pueblo is one of the Tewa towns of Rio Grande pueblos north of Santa Fe, New Mexico; the mountains are considered sacred and are often the home of supernatural beings. In this instance, the Sangre de Cristo Mountains are the sacred focus. For scholars contemporary with Austin, see Pliny Earle Goddard, *Indians of the Southwest* (New York: American Museum of Natural History, 1913) and Elsie Clews Parsons, *Pueblo Indian Religion*, 2 vols. (Chicago: University of Chicago Press, 1939), rpt. Lincoln: University of Nebraska Press, 1996. A more recent discussion is Vincent Scully, *Pueblo: Mountain, Village, Dance*, 2nd edition (Chicago: University of Chicago Press, 1989).

Earth Song

Into the earth my grandfathers dug,
In the palms of their hands they gathered its soil,
In the palms of their hands they gathered its soil,
Into the earth my grandfathers dug,
In the palms of their hands they moistened its soil.
In the palms of their hands they rubbed its soil.

Into the earth my grandfathers dug
The Sacred One, the Ancient One,
Into the earth they dug.
Upon their faces they placed its soil
Upon their foreheads they placed its soil.

Behold it upon my forehead,
The symbol my grandfathers made.
That which I gathered in the hollow of my hand
I put it upon my face and my forehead,
The symbol of the Sacred One, the Ancient One,
The soil of the earth my grandfathers dug,
I put it upon my forehead.

Osage.

Editor's Notes

Austin's note says that "the Osage song is from an initiation rite recorded by Francis La Flesche, and is condensed merely to show the verse progressions controlled by ritual acts." The free translation of the initiation rite, with similar imagery of soil, appears in *36th Annual Report of the Bureau of American Ethnology, 1914–1915* (Washington, D.C.: Government Printing Office, 1921), 170–71.

Star Song

We are the singing stars,
We sing with our light.
We are the birds of fire,
Through the heavens we take our flight.

Our light is as a star,
Making a road for spirits.

Among us are three hunters
Forever chasing a bear.
There never was a time
When they three were not hunting.

We look down upon the mountains.

Passamaquoddy.

Magic Formulas from the Cherokee

Formula for Securing Affection

Hearken!

In Alahiyi, O Terrible Woman, hear me!
In Alahiyi, where your rest is, O White-Fire Woman, you
    have drawn close to hear me.

Most Beautiful! Being with you, none are ever lonely.
Instantly, being with you, I also am rendered fireful.
So that none with me shall ever be lonely!

Now you have emblazoned the path of my life,
It shall never be dreary.
You have put my feet in the White way, with no shadow of
    blueness.
You have put my feet in the flame's way,
It shall never be desolate;
You have brought down for me the White way of souls.
There in the midst of earth horizon you have placed me.
I shall stand erect upon the earth
And no one who is with me shall ever be desolate.
Behold, I am comely!
You have put me into the White house, the aura of all
    things desirable!
It moves with me as I move in the midst of it,

And no one with me shall ever know desolation of spirit.
Truly, White-Fire Woman, by your power
You have caused it to be so with me
That I shall never be disconsolate.

Truly, from Alahiyi, you have shadowed the soul of the woman of my desire.
Now the path of her life you have made dreary.
Let her be completely veiled in loneliness.
Set her feet in the blue road;
Bring her soul down to the low places of the earth;
Where her feet are now, wherever she stands let desolation leave its mark upon her.
That she may turn to me; that she may seek warmth of me;
Where she stands let her be marked out for loneliness.

Hah! Woman of my desire!
I belong to the Wolf Clan, that clan which was allotted to you from the beginning.
No one with me is ever lonely in spirit,
For I am in the flame's way. I am well-looking.
Let her put her soul in the center of my soul never to turn away.
In the midst of other men, grant that she shall never think of them.

O desirable woman,
I am of the one clan which was destined for you when the Seven Clans were established.

Where other men are there is no aura of happiness.
They are loathly to you.
The polecat has made them like himself; they are fit only for his company.
They are utterly inconsiderable!

The common possum has made them like himself; they are
fit only for his company:
Turn wholly from them.

The hoarse rain-crow has made them so like himself; they
are fit only for his company:
They are altogether loathsome.

All the seven clans alike are desolating to the spirit.
They have no comeliness,
They are clothed with the leavings of the tribe,
They go about covered with filth.
But I . . . I am ordained to be kin to the fire-flame,
I am white-burning;
I stand with my face to the Sun-Land,
I shall never be desolate!
Behold, how handsome I am,
Wherever I go I am covered with the everlasting aura
of whiteness,
No one with me shall ever be lonely of spirit.

Your soul has come into the very center of my soul
never to turn away.
I take your soul.

Hearken!

Formula for Separating Lovers

Ah, you dweller of the high places,
Blue Hawk, trouble bringer, of the far distant lake,
The blue smoke of tobacco I offer you in recompense!

Ah, now you have arisen;
At once you have come down to me;
You have alighted mid-way between them,
Those two that I have named to you;
At once their souls you have bemused,
At once they have become separated.

I am a man whose soul is white-glowing,
I stand at the sunrise; in me
The fire-sperm shall be proof against desolation of spirit.

This woman is of the Paint Clan, she is called Wayi.
Instantly we shall turn her soul about,
Instantly it shall be accomplished.

We shall turn it about as we go toward the Sun-land.
I am a man who abides in the aura of happiness;
Here where I establish it, her soul shall come close
against mine,
Let her eyes be ever turning to me and watching,
Where my body is there shall be for her no loneliness.

Formula for Fixing Affection

(The following is recited at night, by stealth, whisperingly, over the person whose affections it is desired to secure.)

Yuh! Hah!

Now the souls have come together.
You are of the Deer Clan,
Your name is Ayasta.
I am of the Deer Clan.

(One of the following is recited four times on each one of four consecutive nights.)

FIRST NIGHT

Your body I take, the whole of you.
I absorb it into myself.

SECOND NIGHT

Your flesh I take, the form of you.
I absorb it into myself.

THIRD NIGHT

Your essence I take, the soul of you.
I absorb it into myself.

FOURTH NIGHT

Your heart I take, the affections of you,
I absorb them into myself.

(After each recitation of the above the hands of the performer are held toward the fire and a little ashes, preferably mixed with spittle of the performer, are rubbed gently on the breast of the subject.)

Hearken! Hah!

Now our souls have met, never to part.
You have declared it, O Ancient One Above,
O Black Spider, you have been drawn down from on high,
You have let down your web.

She is of the Deer Clan,
Her name is Ayasta.
You have enmeshed her soul in your web.
You have caused her to know
That where the people of the Seven Clans are coming
and going,
There is never any feeling of loneliness,
Never any desolation of spirit.

Hearken! Hah!

You have covered her over with loneliness;
Her eyes have faded from all she looked upon,

Her eyes have come to fasten on me alone.
Whither can her soul escape!

Let her be sorrowing where she goes,
And not for one night only;
Let her spirit go aimlessly wandering
On a trail that can never be followed.
Never by any soul but my soul.

O Black Spider you hold her in your web,
Never shall she break through its meshes.
What is the name of the soul,
Now they two have come together?
Her soul, it is mine,
They shall never be separated.

Hearken! Hah!

Now you have given heed to me, O Ancient Red-Fire.
O terrible one, dweller in the heart-coal,
Your grandchildren come to the edge of your abiding
 place,
To the fire's edge holding out our hands to you.
You hold them yet more firmly, never to let go your grasp.
O Ancient One, Red-Fire, we two have become one.
The woman has put her soul into our hands.
We shall never let go.
It is accomplished.
Yuh!

Formula for Turning Aside a Storm

Here you come, He-wind,
In your rutting wrath
Trampling and tossing.
Truly, I fear you!
But it is not I you are tracking.
It is your mate, whose footprints
Flash in white riffles of leaves
Up the slope of the mountain.

Follow where I point you,
Where she goes through the tops of the trees,
Where your path leads,
There in the middle air
None shall disturb your mating.
Let your path go
Where the wavy branches meet
On the lofty mountain!

Editor's Notes

All four texts are very close to the free translations published by James Mooney, "The Sacred Formulas of the Cherokees," in *Seventh Annual Report of the Bureau of American Ethnology* (Washington, D.C.: Smithsonian Institution, 1891), 301–97. In her note, Austin credits Mooney but adds, "It was not until I had additional material which I thought would bring out their poetic values that I ventured to restate them, with the help of Leota Harris, a woman of Cherokee descent, who had the formulas almost in the original form from her mother."

Tribal Lays

Kato Creation Myth: A Fragment

Collected by and translated with the help of Pliny Earle Goddard.

The two Surpassing Beings of the Kato, having decided to destroy the first world and recreate a new, first build a new and higher sky to take the place of the one about to be destroyed, having four portals, four supporting columns, the north and south portals for the sun trails, the eastern portal for the clouds, and one in the west for the fog. They then proceed to bring about the destroying Flood.

It was evening, they say,
The world was darkened with rain, they say;
It rained every day.
What is about to happen, the people said,
It rains every day!

Close to the ground the fog spread,
The sky was covered with clouds,
The people had no fire then,
The fires dwindled, they went out altogether;
All the creeks were full,
There was water in the valleys;
The waters encompassed the land.

The Flood is made; I have finished; said the Thunder.
It is made: said Nagaitcho, Let us ascend.

We will ascend to the upper sky, said Nagaitcho,
To the new sky that we have made.
At night, when all is asleep,
To the four-wayed heaven
We will ascend, they said.

Thus when the people slept, the Flood came, they say.
The waters came together everywhere,
There was no dry land left, nor mountains,
Nor were there any rocks standing above the waters,
Trees and grass were not, they say,
Nor any growing things.
Deer were not, nor the round-horned elk,
Grizzlies were not, nor pumas,
Wolves were not, they say,
Nor the small black bears of the brush country.
All these were washed away.
All the fourfooted kind,
Foxes, and grey squirrels, sharp nosed mice, even,
They were washed away.
There were neither ravens nor owls,
Nor orioles nor mocking birds;
The blue heron and the sand-hill crane,
They were all washed away,
The linnets and the meadow-larks,
The waters washed them away.

In the original, the list of animals and birds is indefinitely extended to include all the species known to the recitor. When the list is exhausted, the narrative goes on as follows:

Then the wind was not, they say,
When the waters were over the land,
There was neither frost nor snow;
Neither was there rain, they say,

Nor did it thunder,
When no trees were, to bring the thunder down;
Nor did the lightning appear.
Then clouds were not in the vault,
Nor fog out of the west-way.
Then the stars were not, but dark was;
Darkness, they say, enveloped the waters.

When the waters were over the land,
Then the sun walked not the sky-roads;
The way thereof was utterly dark.
Then the Earth-animal got up in the north,
The surpassing earth-creature
With its long horns, got up;
It walked this way through the deep places,
The water rose to its shoulders.
When it came to the shallows it looked up;
Its horn emerged from the waters;
There is a great ridge there, they say,
Upon which the waters break ceaselessly.
When it came to the middle place, in the east
The earth-animal looked up under the place of the sun-rise;
There is a great land there, they say,
Toward the sky-gate
Where the earth looked up.

Far away to the south it looked up,
It walked under the world surface;
Coming from the north, it walked southward;
There it lay down.
On the earth's head Nagaitcho was carried,
Standing upright, on the earth's head,
To the south he was carried.
Where it lay down, the earth-animal,

Its head he placed as it should be;
Between its eyes grey earth he placed, they say.
With reeds and clay he built up land,
He caused grass and green herbs to stand upright.
The head of earth-animal was buried out of sight.
On each of its horns Nagaitcho spread soil,
The small rocks he piled around them.
Let them be mountains here, he said;
And mountains became.

I am the land maker, said Nagaitcho,
I will go north, he said,
I will go around the land that I have made,
I shall fix it, he said, I shall finish the land.

As he went, he placed mountains about,
He caused the land to stand up against the waters.
Redwoods and pines he placed along the shore,
The fir and the spruce also.
At the tail of the earth in the north
He caused the fir and the spruce to grow;
As he went he looked back and saw them growing.
From the north he put down great rocks,
Over there the ocean beats against them.
He set mountains round about;
This he did continuing toward the south.
He dragged out creek beds with his foot
For the waters to run back off the earth;
He kicked out springs in the hills.
This, he said, will be water for drinking.
All creatures shall drink of it; it shall not be salt.
Of the salty places he said, these will be deer licks.
Where valleys were required for streams to run in,
He set the land on edge.

As he worked with them, the mountains grew,
As he looked behind him Nagaitcho saw them growing;
The redwoods grew very tall.

Let acorns grow, he said, and tan bark oak.
There will be brush on this mountain, he said.
Here many Grizzlies were living.
He made Manzanita and white thorn grow there.
This shall be a valley, he said,
Where deer shall be in great numbers.
White pines and black oaks he stood up,
When he looked back he saw that they had grown,
The mountains loomed up.
He tasted the springs that he had made,
He saw that the water was good.
His dog was with him as he went about the earth,
Drink, my dog, said Nagaitcho,
He himself drank of the water he had made;
Thus it shall be for animals and birds to drink of.
Walk behind me, my dog, said Nagaitcho;
Thus they went about the earth firming it.

He put rocks along the banks of the streams,
White stones he placed along them.
This shall be a small stream, he said,
Minnows and trout shall abound in it.
In this creek there shall be eels living,
Hook-bill and black salmon shall run up in this creek,
Last of all steel-head shall swim up it.

He put down yellow pines and redwoods in one place,
He set small black bears there,
Here the water shall be black,
It shall not be for drinking,

Here owls shall frequent, the screech and the elf-owl.
There shall be sparrow hawks about.

The list continues until the earth is furnished with all varieties of birds and animals.

How will the ocean behave? said Thunder.
The water will rise up in ridges, said Nagaitcho,
It will settle back again,
There will be sand along the water,
On top the sand will glisten;
Old kelp will come ashore,
Old whales will wash ashore there,
Many kinds of fish shall live there,
The people will eat them.

After finishing the new earth, Nagaitcho turns north again.

Walk behind me my dog, he said,
We will look at that which has taken place.
Walk fast, my dog, he said;
They drank of the water that had become,
They saw that it was good.
The valleys had broadened,
The streams were flowing,
Between the trees the brush was growing;
I have made a good earth, my dog, he said.
Acorns grew on the oaks, hazelnuts ripened,
The berries of Manzanita were whitening,
Many deer fed in the meadows.
All things had grown and matured.
We have made them good, my dog,
The mountains have grown up quickly.

The air is warm, my dog,
It is pleasant to live in.

He turned his steps to the north, away from the earth head,
We will go back, my dog,
Look how the mountains have grown!
We are about to arrive, he said,
We are close to home, my dog,
I am about to arrive in the north,
I am about to get back to my home in the north.
He said to himself three times,
I am about to arrive,
It is finished.

Editor's Notes

Austin's source is Goddard, "Kato Texts," *American Archaeology and Ethnology* 5:3 (December 1909): 77–95, 184–91. In her note, she asserts that "this version of their creation myth was built up, with Mr. Goddard's aid, from two fragments secured by him and one collected by the author."

The Children Sing in the Far West, 1928

In 1928 Austin brought out a second book of poems, called *The Children Sing in the Far West*, collecting some of her earliest published poems along with poems she had collected or written in the 1920s. Like both editions of *The American Rhythm*, the 1928 collection presents a range of poems from a variety of times and places. Austin provides a disarmingly simple introduction to the poems in her preface to the volume, printed below: "I made most of the poems in this collection with the help of the children in my school. We had a wonderful time doing it, they because children always love poetry if it has a good rhythm tune and is about something they can understand, and I because I was in this manner let into the secret of how the great Southwest feels to those who have never known any other country." Although several of the poems in the book derive from Austin's years as a schoolteacher in Owens Valley, most are clearly not the work of her pupils, even in collaboration with their gifted teacher. The seventy-three poems appear in seven thematically titled sections, and only a handful of those poems could be argued to evoke "the child's approach and the child's feeling for the movement proper to his thought." In fact, most of the poems are clearly the work of an adult writing for a mixed readership of both young people and adults.

The complex sense of readership in *The Children Sing in the Far West* emerges in several ways. In the section "Songs the Indians Sing," for instance, Austin reprints several titles from the 1923 edition of *The American Rhythm*, and the fourteen poems in the section are closely allied to the "Amerindian Songs" of both editions of *The American Rhythm.* At least ten poems are reprinted from *St. Nicholas*, the "Magazine for Young Folks" edited by her friend Mabel Dodge at the turn of the twentieth century for the publishers of *Century* magazine. These are some of Austin's earliest magazine publications, dating from September 1900 to June 1904. They are definitely aimed at juvenile readers, and none is challenging in either form or content. On the other hand, several poems are reprinted from adult periodicals like the *Nation*, the *Forum*, and the *Commonweal.* And even though *The Children Sing in the Far West* does not contain a great deal of free verse, poems like the four "Prayers to the Outdoor Saints" in the "Tribal Wisdom" section show how well Austin can use rhyme, stanza, and metrics when she wishes. The twelve-line poem "At Carmel" evokes the poet's sense of place in concise imagery that is both concrete and abstract: "But I go to hear the auklets crying/ Like dark glass on glass" (5–6). Somehow the term *glyph* seems most appropriate here—certainly more accurate than calling it a poem for children. *The Children Sing in the Far West* provides a kind of anthology of Austin's poetry from her earliest writings to her mature style. Like the poetry published between 1898 and 1934, in magazines, newspapers, and books, Austin works in a variety of voices and modes, and she seems to have a mixed audience in mind.

Preface

These songs began to be made nearly forty years ago, when the author was young and the West so new that there were no songs about it that children could have for their own. Partly because I was teaching school and felt obliged to have something for my pupils about the land they lived in, and partly because I loved the land so much I couldn't bear not having grown up in it, I made most of the poems in this collection with the help of the children in my school. We had a wonderful time doing it, they because children always love poetry if it has a good rhythm tune and is about something they can understand, and I because I was in this manner let into the secret of how the great Southwest feels to those who have never known any other country. So I have gone on adding to this list from time to time, hoping that I was still keeping the child's approach and the child's feeling for the movement proper to his thought. All this time I have been waiting for a poet to come along and do for all Western children what I tried to do for those that were in my hands. It is only now that it seems certain no such poet will arrive in my time, that I have decided to publish selections from the verses that were begun so happily by myself and the children at Lone Pine so long ago. In this I have been partly persuaded by the children of those children and their children. To all others who wish to come into touch with the great West by the children's road, they are hopefully offered.

Mary Austin

Acknowledgments are hereby made to St. *Nicholas*, *the Youth's Companion*, *Outing*, *Sunset* magazine, *The American Boy*, the *Commonweal*, the *Nation*, *Everygirl's* magazine, and the *Forum*, in which periodicals many of these verses first appeared.

Thanks are also due to my friend Arthur Davison Ficke for assistance in selecting and editing the present volume.

Songs of the California Coast

Wind Song

Blow in, blow in, O Western Wind!
From out the blue, foam-flowered main,
Blow in across the coastwise hills
And bring the ploughing rain!

Blow, Wind, and stir the yucca spears
To give their tall white candles room,
Blow out the painted poppy cups
And bid the lupines bloom!

Blow in, blow in, O willful Wind,
And whip the drowsy trees,
Shake all their silken tassels out
And wake the humming bees!

Blow up, blow up the summer stars
Hiding the sea rim under,
Blow up the shimmer on warm seas
And the Spring wonder!

The Sandhill Crane

Whenever the days are cool and clear
The sandhill crane goes walking
Across the field by the flashing weir
Slowly, solemnly stalking.
The little frogs in the tules hear
And jump for their lives when he comes near,
The minnows scuttle away in fear,
When the sandhill crane goes walking.

The field folk know if he comes that way,
Slowly, solemnly stalking,
There is danger and death in the least delay
When the sandhill crane goes walking.
The chipmunks stop in the midst of their play,
The gophers hide in their holes away
And hush, oh, hush! the field mice say,
When the sandhill crane goes walking.

Editor's Notes

Published in *St. Nicholas*, according to a reprint in an undated *Shields'* magazine (*AU* 130), but I have not been able to find the poem.

The Blue Crane

Whenever the days are fine and clear
The tall blue crane goes walking
Across the fields by the flashing weir
I see him solemnly stalking
The little frogs in the tules hear
And jump for their lives when he comes near
The little fish scuttle away in fear
When the tall blue crane goes walking

The field folk know when he comes that way
Slowly solemnly stalking
There is danger and death in the least delay
When the tall blue crane goes walking
The chipmunks stop in the midst of their play
The gophers hide in their holes away
And hush O hush the field mice say
When the tall blue crane goes walking

Editor's Notes

An early manuscript poem, in *AU* 182.

Rathers

I know very well what I'd rather be
If I didn't always have to be me!
I'd rather be an owl,
A downy feathered owl,
A wink-ity, blink-ity, yellow-eyed owl
In a hole in a hollow tree.
I'd take my dinner in chipmunk town,
And wouldn't I gobble the field mice down,
If I were a wink-ity, blink-ity owl,
And didn't always have to be me!

I know very well what I'd like to do
If I didn't have to do what I do!
I'd go and be a woodpecker,
A rap-ity, tap-ity, red-headed woodpecker
In the top of a tall old tree.
And I'd never take a look
At a lesson or a book,
And I'd scold like a pirate on the sea,
If I only had to do what I like to do,
And didn't always have to be me!

Or else I'd be an antelope,
A pronghorned antelope,
With lots of other antelope
Skimming like a cloud on a wire-grass plain.
But if I were an antelope,
A bounding, bouncing antelope,
You'd never get me back to my desk again!

Or I might be a puma,
A singe-colored puma,
A slinking, sly-foot puma

As fierce as fierce could be!
And I'd wait by the waterholes where antelope drink
In the cool of the morning
And I do
                    not
                              think
That ever any antelope could get away from me.

But if I were a hunter,
A red Indian hunter,—
I'd *like* to be a hunter,—
I'd have a bow made of juniper wood
From a lightning-blasted tree,
And I'd creep and I'd creep on that puma asleep
And I'd shoot him with an arrow,
A flint tipped arrow,
An eagle feathered arrow,
For a puma kills calves and a puma kills sheep,
And he'd never eat any more antelope
If he once met up with me!

Editor's Notes

Published in *Bookman*, November 1928, 272–73, as part of the article, "Poetry in the Education of Children."

Austin's notes: "Wire-grass is the short, wiry grass that covers all the high plains of the west. It turns yellow early and stands stiffly up in all weathers. Once it was a sure sign of antelope country.

Juniper wood from a lightning-blasted tree. The California Indians think that wood from a tree killed by lightning makes better bows than any other. It is more elastic and lasts longer."

The Sea Marsh

The sea marsh out by Green Brae
Creeps in among the sedges,
A slow tide, a slack tide,
To stir the samphire weed.
Blue herons go a-fishing there;
The wind that drags the edges
Blows in along the shallow pools
The wastrel gulls to feed.

Editor's Notes

Austin's note: "Samphire is the green and reddish weed that covers the salt water marshes from the southern end of San Francisco Bay to the Salinas River, and many other places, making them look like a gay Oriental rug."

Dormidera

Dormidera, Dormidera, the trails are dim with rain,
The herd dog minds the homing flock, the water sings again;
Blue between white shores of cloud, the sky is like a lake,
Spring signals down the orchard row in every rosy flake,
Sweet sap creeps up the almond boughs, oh, Golden-eye awake!

Dormidera, Dormidera, the fumbling sea fog seeks
Round the low fronts of seaward hills, by brown, abounding creeks,
By deer walks, and by faint old trails where once the Padres trod;
On seaward slopes the strong young sun has waked the glowing
    sod.
What dream you, Dormidera, that are so long anod?

Time yet to doze through dripping dawns until you hear the lark,
The nights of spring for dreaming long, the soft owl-haunted dark,
Or when the wind is on the hill to wild oat pipes a-croon
Yet may you lap your tender leaves by full and flooding moon,
But oh, the spring is all to seek unless you waken soon!

Editor's Notes

Austin's notes: "This is a Spanish word meaning 'sleeper,' given to the yellow California poppy because of its habit of staying curled up except when the sun shines brightly. . . . The Padres. The Franciscan monks who founded the Missions of California."

At Carmel

There are people go to Carmel
To see the blue bay pass
Through green wave to white foam
Like snow on new grass.
But I go to hear the auklets crying
Like dark glass on glass.

I go to hear the herons talk
The way that herons have, half asleep,
As they come in past Carmel bar
With a slow wing sleep;
To hear the wood teams jingling up the Sur,
And the contented blether of the Mission sheep.

Editor's Notes

Austin's note: "Auklet, a small sea-bird whose cry is seldom heard until after dark."

The Shepherd Wind

The wind is the shepherd who drives the clouds
    Across the field of the sky,
And fast or slow, as the wind may blow,
    I watch his flocks go by.

His folds are under the rim of the world
    North, south, and east and west—
And the shepherd cares for all of his sheep
But he loves the lambs the best.

In clear, smooth paths of the middle sky,
    And highest up in the air
He lets the snow white cloudlings run
    Whenever the days are fair.

The mother clouds on the mountain browse,
    Or nose along the hill,
Or sleep in the shade of the tallest peaks
    When the shepherd wind is still.

The cloudkins come at his lightest call,
    And he whistles the mothers home,
But he shouts aloud at the black storm cloud,
    For black sheep love to roam.

If ever the tale of the flocks is short,
    Or the shepherd miss his sheep,
He calls by the folds where the white fogs lie
    And whips them out of the deep.

Last night when the gates of the west were ajar
    To let the sun slip through,

I saw the little clouds scampering far
        Into the open blue.

And every one had a golden fleece,
        But a few turned rosy red
As they huddled down the coast-wise hills
        Where willful black sheep led.

While all night seeking his truant sheep
        The whistling wind went by;
He found them at last on the edge of dawn
        Under the lee of the sky;

He drove them back by the shouldering hills
        That fence the great sea lane,
I heard the beat of their scampering feet,
        But others thought it was rain.

And we can follow the way he took
        To the pastures of the deep
For every hill has a snowy fleece
        It stole from the truant sheep.

Editor's Notes

Austin's note: "The 'tale' of the flocks is the account the herders keep. It is an old English word from which our word 'tally' is taken."

The Deer-Star

Hear now a tale of the deer-star,
        Tale of the days agone,
When a youth rose up for the hunting
        In the bluish light of dawn—
Rose up for the red deer hunting,
        And what should a hunter do
Who has never an arrow feathered,
        Nor a bow strung taut and true?
The women laughed from the doorways, the maidens mocked
        at the spring;
For thus to be slack at the hunting is ever a shameful thing.
The old men nodded and muttered, but the youth spoke up
        with a frown:
'If I have no gear for the hunting, I will run the red deer down.'

He is off by the hills of the morning,
        By the dim, untrodden ways;
In the clean, wet, windy marshes
        He has startled the deer agraze;
And a buck of ten-point antlers
        Streams out from the fleeing herd,
And the youth is apt to the running
        As the tongue to the spoken word.
They have gone by the broken ridges, by mesa and hill and swale,
Nor once did the red deer falter, nor the feet of the runner fail;
So lightly they trod on the lupines that scarce were the flower-stalks
        bent,
And over the tops of the dusky sage the wind of their running went.

They have gone by the painted desert,
        Where the dawn mists lie uncurled,
And over the purple ranges
        On the outer rim of the world.

The people shout from the village,
And the sun gets up to spy
The royal deer and the runner,
Clear shining in the sky.
And ever the hunter watches for the rising of that star
When he comes by the summer mountains where the haunts of the red deer are,
When he comes by the morning meadows where the young of the red deer hide;
He fares him forth to the hunting while the deer and the runner bide.

Editor's Notes

Published in *St. Nicholas*, February 1901, 291–92.

Austin's note: "The Paiute Indians tell this story of the bright star which may be seen in the eastern sky just before sunrise of summer mornings, known as Sirius in the constellation Canis Major, also called the 'dog star.' The Paiutes, who live along the western edge of California and in Nevada, say that the best time to hunt deer is when this star is in the sky, which is really true."

Furryhide and Glitterskin

Round about the choyital
Where the blue-throat lizards run,
Hoots the elf-owl from his burrow,
Squats the horned toad in the sun;
Where the glossy greasewood twinkles
And the mesquite dunes begin,
They have made their summer dwelling,
Furryhide and Glitterskin.

It has dark and winding hallways
And a chamber low and wide,
Walls and floors all smoothly patted
By the feet of Furryhide.
It has seven doors of exit
And not one the rain comes in,
But no doorway in that dwelling
Is too small for Glitterskin.

Dark those doorways and deserted
In the blinding desert noon,
But when night-jars chirr and hurtle,
When up comes the mesa moon,
Furryhide goes whisking, frisking,
Dancing with his fairy kin,
Gathering mesquite, nibbling grass seeds;—
Not a stroke does Glitterskin.

When the morning sun has warmed him,
And the kin of Furryhide
Sound are sleeping, he comes creeping,
Wicked jaws distended wide.—
Stoop you to the ruined dwelling,
Oh, so cautiously look in,

Red eyed in the dusky doorway,
There is only Glitterskin.

Editor's Notes

Austin's note: "Choyital means a place where the cholla cactus grows. It is sometimes spelled 'chollital,' but as 'cholla' is really pronounced choya all over the Southwest, it seems better to spell it that way. The cholla cactus is also called 'cane cactus' because of its round straight stems. Mesquite is a thorny shrub growing all over the American desert. . . . The pods are sweet and very nourishing. The Indians grind them up and make them into a kind of bread which keeps for a year or two."

Winnedumah

This the tale of Winnedumah
Whom the Paiute clans revere,
But you must not tell the story
When the snakes can overhear,
When the tall grass makes a cover
Where the spotted snakes may hide,
For the snakes are mischief makers,
Double-tongued and evil-eyed.

But when twilights chill and deepen,
When the streams run scant and small,
When the frost has nipped the piñons
And they hear the wild goose call,
When the children by their mothers
Snuggle closer in the byre,
When the young men come from hunting,
And the old men stir the fire;

Then they tell of Winnedumah,
How he lived and what he wrought,
Dealing straightly with his people,
Speaking truth as leaders ought.
Winnedumah and his brother—
Skilled in magic arts was he—
And they taught the Paiute peoples
What a brother's love should be.

When the warlike, fierce Shoshones
Broke their ancient metes and bounds,
Slew the mule-deer, chased the blacktail
On the Paiute hunting grounds,
When they stole the piñon harvest,
Stopped with earth the mountain springs,

Winnedumah put on war paint,
Put on plumes of eagles' wings;

Set his braves to track them featly,
Stalked them as they stalked the deer
By the high and windy headlands
By the passes straight and sheer.
All by night the women watching
Saw their signals in the sky,
Heard by day above the ambush
The beholding eagles cry.

When at last they drew to battle
Sped the fight in valiant part,
'Til about the hour of sunset
Flew a virus-venomed dart,
Struck at Winnedumah's brother—
Vultures wheeling heard the cry,
Heard the death wail, when the Paiutes
Saw their magic-maker die.

Then their hearts were turned to water,
Since no art the healer saves;
Vultures wheeling slow and stately
Saw the fleeing of the braves.
Only Winnedumah lingered,
Standing on the skyline clear;
Lingered, calling for his brother
Who could neither come nor hear.

Lingered, questing through the twilight
Till he found his brother dead,
Saw the black plumes of his warriors
Through the cedars as they fled,
Saw the wattled huts of willow

Huddled in the Paiute town,
Saw the hot-eyed, fierce Shoshones
Come like wolves to pull him down.

Then the faithful Winnedumah,
Owning neither fault nor fear,
Cried to Taupee, god of Paiutes,
Saying, 'Taupee, Father, hear!'
Swift the word sped, swift the answer;
Taupee touched him where he stood,
Changed him to the granite boulder
High above the white-pine wood.

Gray at twilight, white at noonday,
Faithful Winnedumah stands,
But the thieving, fierce Shoshones
Come no more to vex our lands;
For the wrath of Taupee caught them,
Plunging headlong down the hill,
Changed them all to yellow pine trees,
Gnarled pine trees, standing still.

Then the little Paiute children
When the tale is ended quite,
Turn from leaning on their mothers
To look out across the night;
Then they look at Winnedumah
Darkling through the alpen glow;
Then they count the wicked pine trees
Up the stream-side all a-row;

Then they snuggle to their mothers;
Then they huddle in the byre;
Then they hear the back log singing;
Hear the pine sap in the fire;

Hear again of Winnedumah
Whom the Paiute clans revere—
But you must not tell the story
When the snakes can overhear.

Editor's Notes

Published in *Sunset*, June 1904, 101–4; "High above the white-pine wood" is "High above the swathing wood" in the *Sunset* magazine version.

Austin's note: "The Paiutes of Owens Valley in California tell this story about a granite boulder about a hundred feet tall which stands on the crest of the first desert mountain range west of the Sierra Nevadas, opposite Kearsarge Pass."

San Francisco

The cable cars swing up the hill,
The cable cars swing down
And with them swings the roaring trade
Of San Francisco town.

A gull-gray city by the sea
The gray wall-sided warships win,
With sunlight on her windy hills,
And gray fog drifting in.

The tide goes up to Suisun,
The river fumbles at the Strait,
Westward the long Pacific swells
Slip sidling past the Golden Gate.

A green tide flows along the hills
And washes down into the sea,
The shadows of the waiting ships
Are darkly green as any tree.

And when the water lies at ease
And hills and sea melt into night,
With a slow sound the ferries pace
A milky way of light.

Editor's Notes

Suisun refers to Suisun Bay and Suisun Marsh, a shallow tidal estuary to the northeast of the city of San Francisco. The Strait probably refers to the Mare Island Strait, which connects Suisun Bay to the larger San Pablo Bay at the west. The Golden Gate is the strait lying between San Francisco Bay and the Pacific Ocean.

Mountain Songs

Whisper of the Wind

Whisper of the wind along the sage.
Only wait till I can get the word—
Never was it printed in a page,
Never was it spoken, never heard.
Once I thought I had it when the moon
Stood up young and white behind the grass,
Ah, but it was gone again so soon,
On the scented hill I heard it pass!
Whisper of the wind along the sage—
That was it where once the lupine stirred—
At the moth-hour once I heard it plain,
Once. But I forget the very word.

The Deer

Under the pines and hemlocks
So thick the needles lie
You scarcely hear
The shy dun deer
With its young go softly by.
Follow, follow,
By hill and hollow,
The dun buck bells to the doe,
The moon is bright,
And we feed to-night
Where the buckthorn thickets grow.

Under the pines and the hemlocks
The thick, white cloud mists creep,
And drip all down
The needles brown
Where the dun deer lies asleep.
Follow, follow,
By hill and hollow,
The doe to her spotted fawn;
'Tis dark o' the moon,
But day comes soon
For I sniff the breath of the dawn.

Under the pines and hemlocks
Flickers through light and shade
The deer to his lair
In the deep fern there,
Or to pasture in open glade.
Follow, follow,
By hill and hollow,
Dun buck, and fawn and doe.

The sun is high
And by day we lie
Where only the deer must know.

Winter in the Sierras

The pines are black on Sierra's slope,
And white are the curling snows,
The flowers are gone, the buckthorn bare,
And chilly the north wind blows;
The pine boughs creak,
And the pine trees speak
The language the north wind knows.

There's never a track leads in or out
Of the cave of the big brown bear,
The squirrels have hid in their deepest holes
And fastened the door with care;
The gaunt wolf howls,
And the red fox prowls,
As they hunt far down from the lair.

The eagle hangs on the wing all day
For the chance of a single kill,
And the little gray hawk hunts far and wide
Before he can get his fill.
The white flakes sift,
And the snow wreaths drift
To the cañons deep and still.

Editor's Notes

Published in *St. Nicholas*, December 1901, 107.

The Rocky Mountain Sheep

The red deer loves the chaparral,
The hawk the wind-rocked pine;
The ouzel haunts the rills that race
The cañon's steep incline;
But the wild sheep from the battered rocks,
Sure foot and fleet of limb,
Gets up to see the stars go by
Along the mountain-rim.

For him the sky-built battlements,
For him the cliff and scar,
For him the deep-walled chasms
Where the roaring rivers are;
The gentian-flowered meadow-lands,
The tamarack slope and crest,
Above the eagle's screaming brood,
Above the wild wolf's quest.

When in the riot of the storms
The snow-flowers blossom fair,
The cattle get them to the plain,
The howlers to the lair.
The shepherd tends his foolish flocks
Along the mountain's hem;
But free and far the wild sheep are,
And God doth shepherd them.

Editor's Notes

Published in *St. Nicholas*, September 1900, 955.

Standing Guard

FIRST WATCH

When the light is slant and low
And the evening winds are loose,
Then the cowboy slacks his hand,
Tired upon his tired cayuse.
When the windy torrents flow
Down the slopes of purple shadow,
Then the rein drops to the sand
While the hungry cattle go,
Eager cropping in the meadow,
And his yellow camp-fire glow
Through the tender, glooming shadow
Blooms across the darkling land.

In the fore-watch of the night
When awakes no beast or bird,
Wide about the guarding-ground
Mills the stubborn, anxious herd.
When above the dregs of night
In a swirling froth of light
Stars beyond the stars are hiding,
Then the cowboy on his round,
Sings to cheer his lonely riding;
Sings the shapes of fear to flight,
Till some lone coyote hiding
Wakes a chorus to the sound.

SECOND WATCH

In the dusky noon of sleep
When the moaning herd is down,
There's a formless fear that flies

Whimpering round the guarding ground;
There's a viewless fright acreep,
Fit to wake the earthquake thunder
That from plain and plunging steep
Flies along the crouching skies,
From the pounding hoofbeats under:—
Keen the watch the riders keep,
Lest they wake the stampede thunder
And the viewless fear that flies.

There's a flaming planet wheels
In the lagging, lesser hours
When before the early chill
In his seat the rider cowers;
White the morning planet wheels,
Sick for sleep the cowboy reels,
Saddle-weary and yet riding.
When the bedded herd is still,
To its lair the shadow steals
While the sun-dawn smites the hills,
Then the morning freshness heals
All the ills of night-long riding.

Editor's Notes

Cayuse is a colloquial term for an Indian pony or any horse (*Oxford English Dictionary*).

The Brown Bear

Now the wild bees that hive in the rocks
Are winding their horns, elfin shrill,
And hark, at the pine tree the woodpecker knocks,
And the speckled grouse pipes on the hill.
Now the adder's dull brood wakes to run,
Now the sap mounts abundant and good,
And the brown bear has turned with his side to the sun
In his lair in the depth of the wood—
Old Honey-Paw in the wood.

'Oh, a little more slumber,' says he,
'And a little more turning to sleep,'
But he feels the spring fervor that hurries the bee
And the hunger that makes the trout leap;
So he ambles by thicket and trail,
So he noses the tender young shoots,
In the spring of the year at the sign of the quail
The brown bear goes digging for roots—
For sappy and succulent roots.

Oh, as still goes the wolf on his quest
As the spotted snake glides through the rocks,
And the deer and the sheep count the lightest foot best,
And slinking and sly trots the fox.
But fleet-foot and light-foot will stay,
And fawns by their mothers will quail
At the saplings that snap and the thickets that sway
When Honey-Paw takes to the trail—
When he shuffles and grunts on the trail.

He has gathered the ground squirrel's hoard,
He has rifled the store of the bees,
He has caught the young trout at the shoals of the ford

And stripped the wild plums from the trees;
So robbing and ranging he goes,
And the right to his pillage makes good
Till he rounds out the year at the first of the snows
In his lair in the depth of the wood—
Old Honey-Paw sleeps in the wood.

Tamalpais

That mountain there,
That blue encircled mountain,
Tamalpais!
Whenever I see that mountain
I remember what the old men said.

The waters were over the land,
The whirling waters;
The little Duck there,
Keediweh, the little Duck,
Paddling, paddling,
On the cloud encompassed waters.

The sky there, the windy sky
Like a dirty deerskin quiver,
With arrows of lightning,
And Padahoon, the Sparrowhawk
Blown about the sky there.

Then said the Sparrowhawk:
Ho, little brother,
How shall we make land here?

With earth that I shall bring
From underneath the waters,
Said Keediweh, the little Duck,
And you shall build us mountains;
Sky propping hills
That the waters overwhelm not,
Around a space of quietness.

I shall build a ring here,
Said Padahoon, the Sparrowhawk,

Half for you and half for me,
So we shall live in quietness.

Four days the Duck dived,
Four days the Hawk built,
But his thoughts had left the straight road.

High rose the peaks on the side of the Sparrowhawk,
Scamped were the hills he built for Keediweh.
Angry was the little Duck, coming up from diving.
Seized he hold of Shasta peak,
Pulled against the Sparrowhawk,
Tried to pull the ring around,
Making magic medicine, each against the other,
Till the ring was flattened, as to-day you see it,
Till it broke by Tamalpais and the sea came in,
Till the whelming waters threatened.

Stay, said the Sparrowhawk, frightened of the waters,
Biting out the earth ring, throwing bites behind him,
On the high Sierra side still the bites are showing,
Ho, little brother, shall we call a truce between us?

Then said the little Duck,
Here by Tamalpais shall I build my wickiup,
You shall keep the high side,
The bitten side, the dry side,
But everywhere the water goes
On your side or my side,
The whirling whelming waters
That your greediness let in,
There go the duck tribe,
There you find the Keediwehs
There we scorn the hawk tribe and all their kin!

*

Thus do I remember what the old men said.

Editor's Notes

Austin's note: "This story was told me by a Yokut Indian from Kern River, California. The name is said to come from Tamal, the name of an Indian chief, and the Spanish pais, meaning country, but this is not certain."

Mt. Tamalpais (2571 feet) lies just north of San Francisco's Golden Gate. The wickiup is a temporary shelter, constructed of a frame and brush or branches, such as willow or cottonwood, common to nomadic tribes of the Southwest.

Snow

All day the hills a brooding stillness keep,
As one who feels the near approach of sleep,
Whose thought goes straying idly—till it seems
Awake, to touch the borderland of dreams.

There is no wind to bid the pine trees speak,
The white fir drowses by the babbling creek
That in the silence feels itself dismayed,
And like a child, unchidden, but afraid,
Hushes its prattle to a whispered croon.
And everywhere
There is a poignant sense, not felt nor heard,
As if a mighty angel softly stirred
His strong pinions in our upper air.

As yet no wind, but clouds all white and slow,
Blind clouds that halt and fumble as they go,
Touching remembered landmarks, hill and spur,
Hoar pine and sapling, hemlock, spruce, and fir,
By lake and fall, by cañon, rift and scar,
By long dark reaches where the tamaracks are,
Heart sure, and yet, remembering they are blind,
Uplift mute hands the mountain's face to find.

Follows a little darkening of the air,
With cattle gathering on the lower hills
And sparrows querulous of coming ills,
And so day passes ere we are aware.

Rises the wind by night and builds a roof
Wherein his busy hands with warp and woof
Of frost and cloud go swiftly to and fro
Weaving the white pavilions of the snow.

A day and night within his sun-roof tent
Where his blown breath the tent-flaps outward lift,
He shouts and labors in the smothering drift.
A day and night such as brings back the sense
Our fathers had of formless elements
In mortal strivings with the groaning air,
Then like Ithuriel's fabled spear of old
Thrusts in the dawn, steel blue, two-edged with cold,
And lo! a world all white and wondrous fair.

Editor's Notes

Austin's note: "Ithuriel is the angel of dawn, who lets in the morning light by thrusting his spear under the curtain of darkness."

The Coming of the Snow

All day the hills a brooding stillness keep,
As one who feels the near approach of sleep,
Whose thought goes straying idly till it seems,
Awake, to touch the border-land of dreams.
There is no wind to bid the pine tree speak,
The white fir drowses by the chuckling creek,
That in the silence feels itself dismayed,
And like a child, unchidden, but afraid,
It stills its babble to a whispered croon:
And then a little darkening of the noon
And cattle gathering on the lowest hills,
And sparrows querulous of coming ills.

As yet no wind, but clouds all white and slow,
Blind clouds that halt and fumble as they go,
And touch remembered landmarks, hill and spur,
Grey pine and sapling, hemlock, spruce and fir,
By lake and fall, by cañon, rift and scar,
By long dark reaches where the tamaracks are,
Heart sure, and yet remembering they are blind,
Lift up mute hands its wonted face to find;
Pale mist and formless groaning everywhere,
And then a poignant sense, not felt nor heard,
As if a mighty angel softly stirred
His strong, white pinions in our upper air.

Editor's Notes

This manuscript appears in *AU* 81, dated 1894.

The Forest Ranger

The Forest Ranger rides from town
And low his bridle rein hangs down;
The sure foot mule that bears his pack
Jogs on unhaltered at his back;
        But if the jingling spur
Clanks for a moment on the ground
Half in the trail he turns him round
        To crop the tufted grass.

The Ranger strikes the hillward trail
And well his roving eyes avail
To mark what sign of weather bides
Up on the mountain where he rides,
        Or matters gone amiss;
What sapling firs the cattle broke,
What far trailed banners of blue smoke
        Announce forbidden fires.

His work to ward the viewless lines
That guard a thousand years of pines;
From foolish waste and careless fires
Defend the rain-imploring spires
        That throng ascending steeps,
And where the seedling tree uprears
To hide the scar of witless years,
        To stay the ruthless flocks.

His horse he pastures on the sod
Of glacier meadows else untrod,
One day he mends the dizzying trails
Where next the thunderous storm prevails;
        Or be it snow or sleet

Tightens his knees to his horse's sides,
Swims the sharp ford and forward rides,
        So rides he through the rain.

Songs of the Southwest

Western Magic

There are no fairy-folk in our Southwest,
The cactus spines would tear their filmy wings,
There's no dew anywhere for them to drink
And no green grass to make them fairy rings.

But sometimes in a windless blur of dust
The impish twins of War and Chance go by,
Or after storms the Spider Woman mends
With thin drawn cloud, torn edges of the sky.

And there is One who plays upon the flute
In deep rock crevices where springs are found,—
'Twas at To-yallanne they saw him first,—
In April youths are magicked by the sound.

Hot dawns the turquoise horse, Hohano-ai,
Races the sun in dust of glittering grains,
Or round Pelado Peak the Rainbow Boy
Goes dancing with the many-footed rains.

There are no fairy-folk in our Southwest,
But there are hours when prairie-dog and snake,
Black beetle and the tecolote owl
Between two winks their ancient forms will take,

*

Clad in white skins with shell shield glittering
The sun, their chief, the Ancient road will walk,
Half in her sleep the mothering earth
Of older things than fairy-folk will talk.

Editor's Notes

Austin's notes: "The twins of War and Chance belong to the Pueblo Indians of Arizona and New Mexico; their names are Ahayuta and Matsalima. They have the power of changing their size and form at will, and are responsible for much mischief and occasional good deeds. The Spider Woman belongs to all the Southwest. She sits in the sky and spins the threads of cloud that other people call 'Standing Rain.' The one who plays upon the flute has an unpronounceable name. To-yal'lan-ne means Corn Mountain, sometimes called Thunder Mountain, which stands up over Zuni Pueblo in Arizona. Pelado Peak is in the Navajo country, but the Rainbow Boy plays all over the Southwest. Tecolote is a common name in the Southwest for small owls. The sun carries a shield covered with white shell beads such as the desert Indians use for money."

Prairie-Dog Town

Old Peter Prairie-Dog
Builds him a house
In Prairie-Dog Town,
With a door that goes down
And down and down,
And hall that goes under
And under and under,
Where you can't see the lightning,
You can't hear the thunder,
For they don't like thunder
In Prairie-Dog Town.

Old Peter Prairie-Dog
Digs him a cellar
In Prairie-Dog Town,
With a ceiling that is arched
And a wall that is round,
And the earth he takes out he makes into a mound.
And the hall and the cellar
Are dark as dark,
And you can't see a spark,
Not a single spark;
And the way to them cannot be found.

Old Peter Prairie-Dog
Knows a very clever trick
Of behaving like a stick
When he hears a sudden sound,
Like an old dead stick;
And when you turn your head
He'll jump quick, quick,
And be another stick
When you look around.

It *is* a clever trick,
And it keeps him safe and sound
In the cellar and the halls
That are under the mound
In Prairie-Dog Town.

Homesickness

It is sorrow to me not to be there
In the Rio Grande country where I belong,
Not to hear in March the drip of snow water,
To see the willows redden and the river greening,
Nor to watch in April at Peña Blanca
The wild plums blossom in a quick white storm.
Not to see the cut logs leaping
In the summer freshet of Peñasco water,
And the girls at Taos gathering plums in August,
The bent boughs leaning to the strong brown arms.
Sorrow it is not to see the aspen money flying
Like curdled gold strained through the keen bright air,
Or at Chimayó the chile drying
Till the walls of houses all come toward you
With the warm approaching red.
Oh, sorrow any time not to be there
In the Rio Grande country where I was bred!

Editor's Notes

Published in *Forum*, August 1928, 296.

Austin's notes: "Peña Blanca means White Rock. Peñasco Water means Rocky Creek. Taos is the name of the most Northern Pueblo; the meaning is not known. Chimayó, once an Indian Pueblo, is now a New Mexico town which is famous for blankets made there."

Texas Trains and Trails

Whenever I ride on the Texas plains
I never hear the couplings cluck,
I never hear the trains
Go chuck-a-luck, chuck-a-luck, chuck-a-luck,
I never hear the engine snort and snuffle,
I never see the smoke plume, I never watch the rails,
But I see the moving dust where the beef herds shuffle,
And I think I am a cowboy,
A rope and tie 'em cowboy,
Punching Texas longhorns
On the Texas trails.

And the engine goes *Whoop!*
Whoopee, whoopala!
And the cars go *Ki-yi,*
Ki-yi, ki-yi, coma-la ky-yi,
                    Whoopala,
Ki-yi!
                    Whoop!

No, I never hear the bell, nor the brakeman call
When I ride on the Texas trains;
But I hear the steers bellow and the yearlings bawl,
And the lone wolf howl on the wire grass plains.
And I never play I'm fireman, nor anything like that,
For I'm playing I'm a cowboy,
A bronco-bustin' cowboy,
Riding Texas longhorns
In a ten-gallon hat.

And the trains go *Youpi-ya,*
Get a-long, dogies,
Get a-long, get a-long

Youpi-yi, youpi-ya,
Youpi-youpi-youpi-ya
Get a-long, get a-long,
Youpi-ya,
Yo-o-u-u-p!

Editor's Notes

Published in *Bookman*, November 1928, 275, as part of the article, "Poetry in the Education of Children."

Austin's note credits Newton Gains, "of Christian University at Fort Worth, Texas," for arranging the refrains, which are taken from "well-known cowboy songs, which were mostly made to sing on horseback, as you can tell by trying them yourself at a lope, a trot, or a slow walk." She also glosses *dogies* as "calves recently separated from their mothers."

The Coyote and the Carrion Crow

At the end of the barley harvest when the foothill pastures
fail,
When the streams are stopped at their fountains and the
dry, hot winds prevail,
Then the hungry herds of the southland go up by the mesa trail.
To the snow-fed northern pastures the crawling dust heaps go,
And the gray coyote scents them afar and signals the carrion crow.

Wing up, wing up, O carrion crow,
And tell me what you see!
(He will not venture a needless quest
For a lazy whelp is he.)

Oh, bellow and bleat, and pounding feet,
And heaving flanks I spy,
And some they lag at the herder's word,
And some are like to die.
Oh, long, long, long is the northland trail
And the pace they keep is slow,
And the bunch grass withers by hill and swale;
Ho, ho! said the carrion crow.

There is only his tilting shadow to temper the desert sun
Where the hot air whirls in the hollows and the little dust
devils run,
And never a rill of water, and never a sound but one;
'Tis the howl of the gray coyote far back on the mesa path,
And the cattle paw in the bitter dust and bellow their fear
and wrath.

Wing up, wing up, O carrion crow,
And bring true word to me!

(He will not go where the herders spy
For a skulking thief is he.)

'Tis shambling feet, and dust they beat,
And nostrils wide and red,
And a white hot wind comes out of the south
To drive in the herders' stead.
But long, long, long is the northland trail,
And well do the herders know
Who goes full fed when the cattle fail;
Ho, ho! said the carrion crow.

Trail up by the wind-scoured gullies, by the craters scarred and high,
By the grudging rill of the Bitter Spring where the heedless drink and die,
By the shallow, lineless valleys, and blank, wide wall of the sky.
And over the trudging cattle flaps ever the carrion crow,
And out and aside in the cactus scrub the slinking, sly feet go.

Drop down, drop down, O carrion crow,
Drop down to the feast with me,
(If he knows where his wit may save his skin
There are none so bold as he.)

And it's but to lurk till the yellow murk
Is laid in the wind's long wake,
And we who have ward of the desert lands
Of the desert our fee will take.
Oh, late, late, late comes the mesa moon,
But we sleep full fed I trow,
And the blue white dawn comes hot and soon—
Good sport! said the carrion crow.

Editor's Notes

Austin's note defines carrion crow as "larger and glossier than the common crow."

A Feller I Know

His name it is Pedro-Pablo-Ignacio-Juan-
Francesco García y Gabaldon,
But the fellers call him Pete;
His folks belong to the Conquistadores
And he lives at the end of our street.

His father's father's great-grandfather
Was friends with the King of Spain
And his father peddles hot tamales
From here to Acequia-Madre Lane.

And Pete knows every one of the signs
For things that are lucky to do,
A charm to say for things that are lost,
And roots that are good to chew.

Evenings we go to Pedro's house
When there's firelight and rain
To hear of the Indians his grandfather fought
When they first came over from Spain.

And how De Vargas with swords and spurs
Came riding down our street,
And Pedro's mother gives us cakes
That are strange and spicey and sweet.

And we hear of gold that is buried and lost
On ranches they used to own,
And all us fellers think a lot
Of Pedro-Pablo-Ignacio-Juan-
Francesco García y Gabaldon.

Editor's Notes

Published in *Bookman*, November 1928, 274.
Austin's notes: "De Vargas was the name of the Spanish general who reconquered New Mexico after the Indians had revolted against the Spanish, and in 1680 killed or drove out all the Spanish settlers. De Vargas re-entered Santa Fe, September 5, 1698, and that date has since been celebrated by a fiesta in Santa Fe as De Vargas Day. Tamales are a delicious food made of chicken, corn meal, raisins, olives, chile pepper and spices, rolled and tied in corn husks and boiled. Acequia Madre means mother-ditch and is the large ditch by which water for irrigating is taken directly out of the river."

Elf Owl

Elf owl, elf owl, what do you see,
All day winking and blinking?

I see the smut-nosed badger run
And the rattlesnake coiled asleep in the sun
And the gray coyote slinking.

Elf owl, elf owl, what do you hear?

I hear the nighthawk chirring,
The horned toads scuttering past in fear,
And the rabbit squeal where the red fox is stirring.

Elf owl, elf owl, what do you do
When all of us are sleeping?

I go down to the water hole to wait
Where the frisk tailed things come creeping,
And the little gray mice by the grass stalks climb
To the moon of the mesa, and bide my time
To mark the blind mole's furrow.
And I strike my kill,
And eat my fill,
And get me back to my burrow.

Editor's Notes

Austin notes that the "little ground owl of the Southwest" is "sometimes called 'burrowing owl' because it likes to make its nest in the abandoned burrows of prairie dogs, gophers, and other small ground-living animals."

The Grand Cañon

Now I know what becomes
Of the many-colored days,
Rose yellow evenings,
Red mornings and the hours
When all the hills
Are low and round like grapes
Amber and purple juiced,
And the leaf-colored earth
Pulses with light like sap.
Now I know where they go,
Touching Sandia, Jemez, and San Francisco peaks,
Wing and wing to the west.
They are on their way to the Grand Cañon.
There they lie, overlapping
In motionless unreality.
And all the dim blue dawns,
The lost twilights, hyacinth-hued,
Cuddle down in the cleft,
Old as the world
And all its many-colored days.

Editor's Notes

Place names evoke pueblos near Santa Fe, New Mexico, and the mountains north of Flagstaff, Arizona.

In Papagueria

Very far there
In Papagueria
Stands ocotillo, the torch flower.
It is swaying to the wind's song,
On the tips of its tall stems,
Like a scarlet bird
It dips and rises,
Like the bird's mate, dim breasted,
Its shadow follows
Delicately over the yellow sands.

Very far there, the bisnaga,
The great barrel cactus
Is swelling with the summer rains.
Leaning always toward the sun,
Clockwise its shadow goes,
While the young men gather bisnaga blossoms
For their maidens to fasten in their hair;
They are singing, 'What are bisnaga spines to me
Whom love is forever pricking in the side!'

Very far, in Papagueria
It stands, the sahuaro,
In its arms there, the red hawk's nest.
The blue lizards and the woodpeckers
Are running up and down.
Would I were there now,
Gathering crimson sahuaro fruit
For the syrup-making,
Drinking sahuaro wine with the old men,
Prayer feathers fluttering.
Would I might hear again

The night-singing mockingbird
Climbing up and down his ladder of sound.

Editor's Notes

Published in *Nation*, July 18, 1928.

Austin's note: "Papagueria is the country of the Papago Indians, south of the Gila River in Arizona, extending down into Mexico." She notes that *Land of Journeys' Ending* (1924) has a whole chapter on the cacti, saguaro wine, and ladder of song. "Bisnaga is the large barrel-shaped cactus of which cactus candy is made." Gary Paul Nabhan describes the Papago ritual of drinking fermented saguaro cactus juice for calling down the rain in *The Desert Smells Like Rain* (Tucson: University of Arizona Press, 1982). The current name used for Papago Indians is Tohono O'odham.

The Rhyme of the Pronghorns

This is the tale that the howlers tell
At the end of the hunting weather,
When the quick rain rills
On the bare, burnt hills,
And they talk in the lair together.
Gray coyote and lean gray mate
And little gray cubs that cry
When the wet wind shrills
In the lone, waste hills,
And the rains go roaring by.

Now this is the law the pronghorn makes
For himself and the fawn and the doe,
When the rank wild oats are belly-deep,
And the waning poppies blow:
The young must run at the mother's flank,
But the bucks they run alone
From the time the old year's horns are cast,
Till the new year's horns are grown.

And up they go by the tumbled hills
Where the windy mesas lie,
And the black rock slips from the ruined lips
Of the craters stark and high;
And far they range, and fast they run;
But the howlers mark them go.
Oh, still and fleet are the padding feet,
And many a trick we know!

We bay them down from the feeding-ground,
We fend them back from the pool,
And ever we raise the hunting howl
When the sun-warmed mesas cool.

And well they need both wind and speed
When the gray coyote pack,
By twos and threes from the hidden hills,
Breathes hot on the pronghorn's track.

Oh, the red hawk knows where the gophers run,
The mice hear the elf owl call,
The badger hunts for the squirrel hills;
But man he hunts for us all.
And he has taken the pronghorn doe
And the buck with his gun and his snare;
He has set him a price on the howler's skin,
And tracked us home to the lair.

And now we lurk in the scrub by day,
And now we slink in the dark;
And only the foolish rabbits quake,
And only the squirrels hark.
And we must bark at the mesa moon,
And round by the sheep-folds prowl,
With never a kill that is worth our skill,
To raise at our hunting howl.
And we must eat of the sun-dried meat
Of the herds when the pastures fail,
And we who were lords of the mesa-lands
Must skulk from the white man's trail.

Gray coyote and lean gray mate
And little gray cubs that bark,
Hearing the tale that their fathers tell
Up in the lair in the dark.

Editor's Notes

Published in *St. Nicholas*, January 1901, 214–16.

Austin's note says the pronghorn used to be plentiful but that "there are but a few of them left now, and these are protected by law from men hunters, but no law can protect them from coyotes, who hunt them by relay races, for no one coyote is able to run down an antelope." See Austin's short story, "The Last Antelope," published in the *Atlantic*, July 1903, 24–28, and collected in *Lost Borders* (1909).

All Outdoors

Showers

The showers race across the sky
To make the hilltops green,
The wind must blow them twenty ways
To wash the willows clean.

The spent drops twinkle in the grass
And mirror pools thread every lane,
While feather-wet the meadow lark
Is singing in the rain!

The Beggar Wind

In winter when the nights are long
The beggar wind goes crying,
And seeks above the shallow ponds
In midland pastures lying.
He whines above the dozing marsh
And through the orchards shivers,
He frets the leafless poplar row
And whimpers to the rivers.

O kindly waters, give, he cries,
A-cold and still imploring,
To warm me give your garnered heat
The summer heat you're storing.
And so he wheedles beggar wise
As through the dark he shivers,
So takes their dole and leaves behind
The ice on lakes and rivers.

Spring in the Valley

When the catkin's on the willow
        And the tassel on the birch,
The wild bees from the hiving rocks
        Begin their honey search.
Brown wings among the browner grass
        And breast all brightening yellow—
Pipes up from meadows as we pass
        The lark's call, clear and mellow;
Now wakes the burnished dragonfly
        Beside the glinting river,
That shakes with silent laughter where
        The iris banners quiver;
Now on the budding poplar boughs
        The tuneful blackbirds perch:
For the catkin's on the willow
        And the tassel on the birch!

Now stalks the solemn crow behind
        The farmer in the furrow;
The downy owl comes out at dusk
        And hoots beside his burrow.
Now blows a freshening wind at morn
        To call men to the sowing;
Now all the waterways are full,
        And all the pastures growing;
Now truant anglers drop a line
        To catfish and to perch:
For the catkin's on the willow,
        And the tassel on the birch!

Editor's Notes

Published in *St. Nicholas*, May 1903, 589.

Sea Gulls

When the tides are full
'Tis the daring gull
Rides out the toiling sea;
When the tides are out
We scrabble and shout
Where the warring breakers flee;
When the sea squall whips
The staggering ships
There is sport for such as we.

For all our brood
The sea has food,
We gather where we may,
In the long white wake
The ferries make
Plowing the windy bay,
In the wasteful slack
Where the tides turn back
And the rivers bar the way.

But most we seek
Some rock shore bleak
Where hoarse sea-lions cry,
On the salt rimed edge
Of a sunless ledge
As the ravening surf goes by;
For such as we
Is the wrack of the sea;
We are wards of the deep and the sky.

Indian Giving

O Sea that eats the land!
Round about the earth rim going,
Hollow maw and clutching hand,
With no halting in your flowing;
You that lap the slope and field
In the silt of creek and river,
Food that summer freshets yield—
You are but an Indian Giver!

Once you gave the lands to men—
Sea marks yet the hills are showing—
Will you have them back again,
Now you see how fair they're growing?

Blue-Eyed Grass

Blue-eyed grass in the meadow
And yarrow white on the hill,
Cat-tails that rustle and whisper
To a wind that is never still;

Blue-eyed grass in the meadow,
And a laden bee's low hum,
Milkweed that runs to be first in the field
Before the butterflies come;

Watersnakes making lacy rings
Round a cardinal-flower's red spear,
And blue-eyed grass in the meadow
To mark the noon of the year!

Editor's Notes

Published in *St. Nicholas*, June 1904, 703; the magazine version is similar to the first and second stanzas here, without a third stanza.

The Black Brant

By the level whispering beaches
Where a sea arm inland reaches
        And the clacking gulls careen,
Where at bar the long surf grumbles
And the sea wrack rolls and tumbles,
        Feed we, tide and tide between.

When the cranes go northward yearly,
When the geese honk high and clearly,
        And the plover calls the rain,
Where the sea rim glints and glimmers
And the moon path to it shimmers,
        Get we darkling to the main;

From the ice-blink on the edges
Of the stark, wind-driven wedges
        That divide the Northern seas,
Sea birds of the shining feather,
Flock we craftily together
        Where the pirate fulmar flees.

When the beach birds beat to cover,
Willet, sanderling, and plover,
        With our singing wings aslant,
Seek us in the high tide hollows
Where the stinging sea spume follows,
        We the sea kings, we the Brant!

Editor's Notes

There are several manuscript versions of this poem, as well as typescripts and offprints from a magazine publication, possibly *St. Nicholas*. See *AU* 381 and *AU* 555.

Clocks and Calendars

What need has he of clocks who knows
When highest peaks are gilt and rose
Day has begun,

Or if the sun
Wears for that day his mask of cloud
Beneath it sees,—
Black wings barred white for day and night,—
The magpies in the piñon trees
Shouting the hour aloud;
Or who has found
High in the blue above the peaks
The sign he seeks,
Of buzzards making a merry-go-round?

What need of hours for whom
The mountain shadow marks the noon,
That straight begins to run
East from the mountain's foot against the sun;
For whom the turn from noon to afternoon
Is set by cattle underneath the trees,
Shut-eyed against the heat-dance on the plain?

What dial prompter than the hour
The red hawk hunts on the mesa trail,
Or down to the water hole troop the quail,
Or the small pale moons of the gilia flower
Open against the level light?
And all the solemn night
The stars go clockwise round the Pole.

What use has he for calendars
Who notes the yellowing junipers

Grow suddenly taut and bright;
Who knows it is March when the eagles mate,
And June when he finds at the water gate
Yellow scum of the pollen of pine
Which the sheep men take for a sign
That the passes are cleared and the lake trout bite;
Or who plants his corn when the scrub oak leaf
Is little and furred like a mouse's ear,
And when blue butterflies appear
Lays it by for the year?

Let me be one who never cares
A fig for clocks and calendars,
But with never a hurry and scarcely a fear
Lives by the signs of the day and the year.

Editor's Notes

Austin's note: "The white bars in the Magpies' wings are called 'footsteps of morning' by the Indians because these birds are usually seen very early in the day."

Lighthouse and Whistling Buoy

The sea-sand drifts about my feet and whitens on the dunes,
While, still complaining to the sky, the rocking water croons;
The salt, salt spray blows in by day, by night the breakers roar;
The white sea-horses toss their manes, all trampling on the shore.

All hours I hear the whistling-buoy across the long tides cry,
And watch the smoke of steamships trail along the down-bent sky,
And see the fog-bank mountains build, or doze and dream all day,
Or count the sails of fisher-boats, or watch the porpoise play.

But night at last steals down the sky, and be it late or soon,
And be the ocean inky black or whitening to the moon,
Or ruffling to a quiet wind or storm lashed, breaking high,
All night on all its changing moods I keep a watchful eye.

And coastwise throw a steady beam, by which the good ships steer;
And meanwhile sounds the whistling-buoy to bid them not come
near.
We have the trade of states to guard, and lives of sailor-men,
And sleep not till the screaming gulls call up the day again.

And when the little fisher-boats come beating up the bay,
We call them in by pier and port, or bid them sheer away,
So up and down our coasts they ply, and fear its reefs no more
While whistling-buoy and lighthouse keep their watch along
the shore.

Editor's Notes

Published in *St. Nicholas*, October 1902, 1059–60.

Santa Maria de Todo el Mundo

Feliciano, our sheep herder says—
And Jose Maria, tie cutter for the Denver and Rio Grande
        railroad says too—
That he lives at Santa Maria de Todo el Mundo,
Which is the same as saying that his home is
Wherever he hangs up his hat.

It is saying that he goes where the trail goes,
That he takes what he finds with only liking for a reason,
Young quail in the garramboya,
Pitahayas and piñon nuts in season.
It's saying he doesn't come in when it rains
But curled up in his poncho wakes to hear it
Pattering on the close piled aspen eaves;
Or the puma by the deer's half-eaten carcass
Screams in triumph as he leaves,
Or the bluebird wakes him with notes new-washed
        and rounded
And a bright wet wing.

It's saying that he works for other men
But when the work is done there's nothing binds him,
Nothing over, like lessons taken home from school.
He keeps his axes sharp
Or makes his herd dogs mind him,
And for the rest he lives by liking, not by rule.

And I say to myself, there's one thing certain,
Whatever comes, I'll save some days to live like that,
At Santa Maria de Todo el Mundo,
Wherever I hang up my hat.

Editor's Notes

Austin's note: "When people in the Southwest are asked where they live, and do not have any settled home, or, if they think it is none of your business, they answer that they live at Saint Mary's of the Whole World. Garramboya is a large round stiff bush that the quail build their nests under to be safe. Even a coyote is turned back by a garramboya. Pitahaya is a general name for any low-growing cactus with edible fruit."

Tribal Wisdom

Grizzly Bear

If you ever, ever, ever meet a grizzly bear,
You must never, never, never ask him where
He is going,
Or *what* he is doing;
For if you ever, ever, dare
To stop a grizzly bear,
You will never meet *another* grizzly bear.

Dead Water

At midnight drink no water,
For I have heard said
That on the stroke of midnight
All water goes dead.

You may drink the moment after,
Or the moment just before,
But it's better to be cautious
And wait a minute more,

Till the clock has finished striking
And tomorrow is to-day,
Or you'll drink dead water
And wither quite away.

Editor's Notes

Austin's note: "This is a superstition of the little Spanish towns in New Mexico."

Seven Rhyming Riddles

I

I come more softly than a bird,
And lovely as a flower;
I sometimes last from year to year
And sometimes but an hour.

I stop the swiftest railroad train
Or break the stoutest tree.
And yet I am afraid of fire
And children play with me.

II

I being tightly bound
Work the faster,
Being strongly held
Best serve my master.

III

I have no wings, but yet I fly,
I'm slender as a snake and straight as rain,
Who takes me in must die,
Who lets me quickly go will surest gain.

IV

I never speak a word
But when my voice is heard
Even the mountains shake,
No hands I have
And yet great rocks I break.

V

I have a grave and solemn mien,
Yet children laugh wherever I am seen,
Though every Christian grace I lack
I always wear a cross upon my back.

VI

My mouth is always furthest from my head,
I run and run and run,
And yet I'm never done,
And somehow I am always found in bed.

VII

First I leave the little house
That I was born in,
Then I lose my overcoat,
Next I lose my skin.

First I am frosted,
Second, I am beaten,
Third, I am roasted,
Fourth, I am eaten.

Editor's Notes

Austin's note: "I, Snow. II, Water in an irrigating ditch. III, An arrow. IV, Thunder. V, A burro. VI, A River. VII, A piñon nut."

Ishets

If you ever see a beetle,
A shiny black beetle,
An absent-minded beetle,
Standing on his head in the sand,
You should never speak of stars,
Never, O my stars!
Not a word about stars,
You understand!

For the beetles once were people
When the very first people,
The Pima Indian people
Came up from under ground,
And gave Ishets the stars to carry,
The bag of stars to carry,
And told him he must hurry
And set the stars around.

He must set them all in order,
The large stars first in order
And the small stars for a border
All around the edge of night.
He must fasten them securely
So their risings would come surely
With the star beams shining purely
To give the people light.

But Ishets forgot to hold them
As the first, first people told him,
Though he knew that they would scold him
If he let the stars escape.
So in less than half a minute
The star bag had nothing in it,

It had almost nothing in it,
And Ishets was in a scrape.
For the large stars had no order
And there wasn't any border
And Ishets for this disorder
Was in a dreadful scrape.

And that's the reason why
All across the summer sky
Stars in crooked clusters lie
With between them starless spaces,
And that's why, when you go walking,
If the beetles hear you talking
About stars, they hide their faces.
So you must not speak of stars,
You must never say, My stars!
Just to save the beetles' faces.

Editor's Notes

Austin's note: "Millions of these little beetles can be seen standing on their heads in the sand along Southwestern trails. Their name is also Utset and Isheet."

Travel Signs

When you go a-traveling
Early in the morning,
If you see a magpie
Traveler, take warning!
Turn you round straight away
Start again another day.

But if two should be together
In juniper or pine,
Go your way in confidence,
That's a lucky sign!

Charms

I

FOR WALKING

As I walk . . . as I walk . . .
The universe is walking with me . . .
Beautifully . . . it walks before me,
Beautifully . . . it walks behind . . .
Beautifully on every side . . .
As I walk . . . I walk in beauty.

II

FOR GOING A-HUNTING

O my brothers of the wilderness,
My little brothers,
For my necessities
I am about to kill you!
May the Master of Life who made you
In the form of the quarry
That the children may be fed,
Speedily provide you
Another house;
So there may be peace
Between me and thy spirit.

III

FOR KEEPING FRIENDS FAITHFUL

The strength of the vine
It has entered into my saying
        It will twine,
        It will twine,
        Around the heart of my friend.

*

The endurance of the oak
It has entered into my saying
    It will hold,
    It will hold,
    It will hold my friend forever.

The sureness of the sea
It has entered into my saying
    It will turn,
    It will turn,
    However far my friend has wandered
    He will return as the sea turns.

By the strength of the vine
By the endurance of the oak
By the sureness of the sea
By a threefold charm
I have bound my friend to me.

Wise Man

Old Tio Juan is the wisest man that lives;
He works for my father and sometimes talks to me,
'And one "take this" is always better than two "I will gives,"'
Says he.

Or if I am talking, and Tio Juan hears,
Of how silly I think other people can be,
'One donkey calling another Long Ears,'
Says old Tio Juan, says he.

If he sees me being greedy about my pie
Or anything else that's nice,
'Whoever eats and puts something by, spreads the
table twice,'
Says he.

Or if I am telling him something mean
That one of my friends has done to me,
'On the finest cloth the smallest spot is easiest seen,'
Says he.

'A sparrow in the hand,' says old Tio Juan,
'Is better than a vulture on the wing,' says he,
'And better than a friend you can't depend upon
Is an honest enemy.'
For a very wise man is old Tio Juan,
A wise old man is he.

Prayers to the Outdoor Saints

SANTA DOUCELINA

Sweet Saint, whose eyes did see
The peach turn rosy on the tree,
Ripe moons of apricots appear
Through cloudy green,
Or skins of pears grow honey clear,
And at the sight
God's love was round you like a light,
Lady, watch in my orchard here,
It may be I shall see what you have seen!

Lady for whom need only pass
The striped snake in the low grass
Or field mouse squeak behind the plough,
Or any bird
Sing sweetly forth from any bough,
And at the sound
For you God's grace did suddenly abound,
Sweet Saint, walk in my orchard now,
It may be I shall hear what you have heard!

SAN ISIDRO

No bell, but blackbirds call my matin hour,
The brown loam curls before my share,
As I thank God for a ploughman saint
To heed a ploughman's prayer.

I do not, San Isidro, vainly ask
Angels to plough for me as once for you,
But help me drive the ploughshare deep
And hold the furrow true.

*

I do not pray for sudden springs to gush
With welcome water from the sun parched plain
But since on all the rain must fall,
Send us the poor man's rain.

A farmer has so many worrying things
That seem too small for him to ask of God,
To make the corn fill out the tasselling ear,
The beans round out the pod,

To make the cows give down their milk
And keep the prices fair,
But San Isidro, friend and farmer once,
Hearken a ploughman's prayer.

OUR LADY OF GUADALOUPE

Guadalupana,
You who did make
Out of bare rocks
At Tepeyac,
Roses to bloom
For Juan Diego:—
Grant Gracious Lady,
Out of this soil
And my hard labor,
Red rose and yellow
And white with Thy whiteness,
Grant that my pansies,
My zinnias and phloxes
Declare by their brightness
Thy happy appearing,
Like my tall hollyhocks
Statelily walking.
Blue be my larkspurs

As folds of Thy mantle,
Shining my marigolds
As the stars round Thee.
Guadalupana,
Smile on my garden.

SAN FRANCISCO

Saint that in gentleness
With the wild creatures there
Walked in the wilderness,
Preaching to wolf and snake
Kindness for Jesus' sake,
And to birds of the air:
Of thy sweet friendliness
Mine be a share!
Let me not needlessly
Waken to fear of me
Any least thing
That goes with claw or wing,
Squirrel in hollow tree,
Birds in their nest.
Let me not heedlessly
Scare the shy waterfowl
From reedy rest.
And if I cannot preach
God's gracious word
To any beast or bird,
May all God's creatures teach
God's ways to me!

Editor's Notes

"Santa Doucelina" was published in *Commonweal*, July 25, 1928, 313.

Austin's note: "Nothing more is known of Santa Doucelina except that she felt God closer to her when she heard birds sing, or looked on flowers and fruits, than when she was in her cloister. San Isidro was a Spanish farm laborer who spent so much time in prayer that his master complained. Then the angels came and ploughed for him while he prayed. Also he caused water to spring up in a dry year to save the crops. In New Mexico butter is eaten on San Isidro Day, even by the poorest farmer. Among the Spanish-speaking farmers of the Southwest a 'poor man's rain' is one that falls at night. The story of the appearance of Our Lady to a poor Indian at Tepayac can be found in the Encyclopedia. She is very popular in the Southwest. San Francisco. This is the Spanish name of Saint Francis of Assisi. He is the Patron Saint of New Mexico."

Morning Prayer

I arise, facing east,
I am asking toward the light:
I am asking that my day
Shall be beautiful with light,
I am asking that the place
Where my feet are shall be light,
That as far as I can see
I shall follow it aright.
I am asking for the courage
To go forward through the shadow.
I am asking toward the light!

Evening Prayer

O Great Mystery,
My heart is open
Though my mind is sleeping
And my eyes are shut.
Come, Great Mystery,
Into the secret places,
And while my mind is sleeping
My heart be teaching.
Then all day thereafter
My heart shall be remembering
What it knew at night,
And however my thought stumbles
My heart will stand upright.

Songs for Occasions

A Song for Western Men

Come let us sing of Western men,
Stout men and true.
Viva! Whoopla! Hurray!
If it wasn't for fellows like these now and then
What would the rest of us do!

Sing now of Adelantados,
Viva, Whoopla, Hurray!
Of Cabeza de Vaca,
Fray Marco de Niza,
Of Don Fernando de Coronado
And his Spanish gentlemen
God rest their souls.
Amen!

Sing now of Conquistadores,
Viva, Whoopla, Hurray!
Of Don Juan Oñate
The first of our founders
Diego de Vargas who saved the land for us
And their capitans nine and ten,
God bless their work,
Amen!

Sing now of famous trail makers
        Viva, Whoopla, Hurray!
Of Fray Escalante
And fighting Kit Carson,
Of Zebulon Pike and his thousand-mile hike
God send us their like
                                        Again.

Come let us sing of Western men,
Stout men and true.
If it wasn't for fellows like these now and then,
What would the rest of us do.

Editor's Notes

Austin's note: "Viva is the Spanish 'hurrah.' Whoopla is the cowboy way of saying the same thing. There are so many kinds of people in the Southwest that we have to use all the words. Cabeza de Vaca was the first white man to cross this part of the United States. Fray Marco de Niza was a Spanish monk, the first to come up from Old Mexico as far as Zuni. Francesco de Coronado was the first adelantado in charge of an expedition to explore the country as far north as Kansas. An adelantado is the officer who goes before in a new country. Juan de Oñate crossed the Rio Grande in 1598 and founded New Mexico and its capital at Santa Fe. Diego de Vargas brought back the Spanish after the Indians had driven them out. Escalante was a priest who first found a trail from Santa Fe to Monterey, the capital of California. Kit Carson was a noted scout and trapper. Zebulon Pike discovered the mountain in Colorado named after him. All the names in this song are for New Mexico; if you live in any other of the Southwestern States, you must put in the other names for yourself."

Little Songs of Spring

I

Cream-cups, butter-cups,
        Dandelions and sedges;
Blackbirds in the poplar row,
        Sparrows in the hedges;
Fruit-buds in the orchard
        Swelling with the rain;
All the close-fed pasture-lands
        Growing green again.
Poppies on the river-bluff
        Soon will wake from sleeping;
Home along the foothills
        Wooly clouds come creeping.

II

Painted-cup, O painted-cup,
Tell me what you hold!
Just a drop of honey dew
And dust of yellow gold;
For ruby-throat and speckled-wing,
And brown-barred, buzzing bee.
And when they all have had their fill,
The painted-cup for me!

III

Where poppies blow,
Where sunshine melts in soft warm showers
That bluster down the happy vales,
And when the mood of showering fails
Laugh mid the rainbow-tinted flowers

By dim sweet trails.

Where poppies blow,
And sheep across the hilltops graze,
And fishing smacks far out at sea
Mark all their shoreward slopes ablaze,
There would I be,
Where poppies blow!

Editor's Notes

Part I was published as "Signs of Spring" in *St. Nicholas*, April 1903, 494.

Little Songs of October

PIÑONERO

Oh, Piñonero!
Now you are back in the piñon tree,
It means snow on the mountain
And school for me,
Piñonero!
And I wish I had nothing else to do
Than flit about in a coat of blue
Eating piñon nuts,
Like you,
Piñonero!

RABBIT-BRUSH

All down arroyo seco
Where a river should belong,
There's never any river
All summer long.
But as soon as comes October
There's a yellow river flows,
A frothy yellow river,
A money-yellow river
Where the rabbit-brush grows.

HUNTING WEATHER

When misty, misty mornings come,
When wild geese low are flying,
And down along the tule marsh
The mallard drakes are crying;
When cattle leave the highest hills,
And blackbirds flock together—

By all these signs the hunter knows
Has come good hunting weather!

Editor's Notes

"Hunting Weather" was published in *St. Nicholas*, October 1903, 1115.

Austin notes that *piñonero* is the "Western Jay, called in New Mexico and Arizona Piñonero, from his habit of spending the winter in the piñon trees, feeding on the pine nuts which are very good eating." The term *rabbit-brush* applies to several species of shrubby plants that "in autumn burst into bright golden-yellow bloom."

The Shepherds in Judea

O the shepherds in Judea,
They are pacing to and fro,
For the air is chill at twilight,
And the weanling lambs are slow.
Leave, O lambs, the dipping sedges, quit the bramble and the briar,
Quit the fields of barley stubble, for we light the watching fire;
Twinkling fires across the twilight, and a bitter watch to keep
Lest the prowlers come a-thieving where the flocks unguarded sleep.

O the shepherds in Judea,
They are singing soft and low,
Song the blessed angels taught them
All the centuries ago.
There was never roof to hide them, there were never walls to bind,
Stark they lie beneath the star beams whom the blessed angels find;
With the huddled flocks upstarting, wondering if they hear aright,
While the Kings came riding, riding, solemn shadows in the night.

O the shepherds in Judea,
They are thinking as they go
Of the light that broke their watching
On the hillside in the snow.
Scattered snow along the hilltops, white as springtime fleeces are

With the whiter wings above them, and the glory
streaming star;
Guiding star across the house-tops; never fear the
shepherds felt,
Till they found the Babe in manger where the kindly
cattle knelt.

O the shepherds in Judea,—
Do you think the shepherds know
How earth round our hearts are brightened
By the ruddy Christmas glow;
How the sighs are lost in laughter and the laughter
brings the tears
As the thoughts of men go seeking back across
the darkling years,
Till they find the wayside stable that the star-led
Wise-men found,
With the shepherds, mute, adoring, and the glory
shining round.

Editor's Notes

Published in *St. Nicholas*, December 1900, 98–101.

A Child's Night Thoughts

When I go to bed in summer
        It is neither day nor night,
But too dark for any playing,
        And too clear for candle light;
And I watch the weeping willow,
        Like my mother's loosened hair,
Sweeping softly past my window,
        Lifting in the wandering air.

Then I hear the wild things talking,
        From the meadow hear the frogs,
Hear the crickets in the windrows,
        And the far off barking dogs.
Then the bats go swift and stilly
        And the furry moths are free,
And the pale, wide primrose blossoms
        Seem like fairy moons to me.

To some far off starry pastures
        Every cloud the wind has led,
And I go out as the moth goes,
        Though my body lies a-bed;
Just my thought goes out a-roving
        On two flitting, velvet wings,
To be playing in the wood-glooms
        With the soft-foot, furry things.

Goes out softly to the pastures,
        And the pleasant path that leads
By the hang nest in the buckthorn,
        And the teary jewel-weeds;
Goes and sits up where the owl sits,
        Where the fairy field mice creep,

Finds the red fox in the wood-lot,
        And the striped snake asleep.

By and by the moon comes climbing
        Up the long steep wall of sky,
Climbs up slowly by the hilltops
        Where the grass stems rank and high
Stand up black against the moon face
        Like a forest in the sod,
And the moon so white and quiet,
        Makes me somehow think of God.

But when comes no moon at all,
        Just one winking, windy star,
Then I think I should be frightened
        For God seems so very far;
But the frogs keep on all night,
        And a cricket chirps for proof,
And the house seems snug and safe
        When the wind walks on the roof.

Evensong

Rest thee, rest thee, pretty one,
Roaring waves have hid the sun,
Shepherd dogs upon the hill
Pace the flock round, slow and still,
Lest the red-eyed prowler spy them,
Lest the wicked wolf come nigh them.
Till the shepherd's watch is done
Rest thee, rest thee, pretty one!

Rest thee, rest thee, merry maid,
Up the hill-slope creeps the shade,
Now the clovers fold their leaves
Bowed above the blossom sheaves,
At the spring the doves are drinking,
Night-eyed primrose buds are winking
In the pastures where you played.
Rest thee, rest thee, merry maid!

Rest thee, rest thee, happy lad,
Flit the dreams of sports you had
Round the sill and up the stair;
Time to set the dreamland snare.
Till you hear the peewits crying
Dreams of sea and wild wood vying
So to make thy slumber glad;
Rest thee, rest thee, happy lad!

Rest thee, rest thee, pretty one,
Owl that has his song begun
Tells how king and camp and court
For such dreams would leave their sport,
Tells that some are all night weeping

Who would envy this thy sleeping;
Till the sea gives up the sun
Rest thee, rest thee, pretty one!

The Christmas Fir

The wind it wends through the young green leaves,
And a whisper runs in the wood
That whatever has root in the earth believes
That the earth works only good;
And the whole wood knows what virtue goes
To the balsam drip of the pine,
To the oak and the larch, and the elm's broad arch
And the linden's tassels fine.
But vainly flutter the gossip leaves,
And vainly the branches stir
To guess what secret meaning grows
In the whorls of the star-branched fir.

O the gnarly oak grows all abroad,
And the birch is slight and trim,
And the bramble sprawls where the adder crawls
By the slant gray boulders' rim.

But straightly, straightly groweth the fir
Where the white whipped waters are,
Greenly spreadeth her branches new;
And the branches form a star.

There are no two leaves of the oak alike,
And no two chestnut burrs,
But each is a twin of the other one
In the boughs of the silver firs.

And ever the star-form they repeat
With never a slip or loss,
And the smallest twig and the topmost sprig
Of the evergreen firs, is a cross.

*

O the trooping quail go by, go by,
When the shadows are blue and cool,
And the shy brown deer stoop under the boughs
To drink of the still brown pool;

The wind goes quizzing the shambling bears
That harry the hiving bees,
And the little gray hawks that hunt in the gloom
Of the stately, star-built trees.

The small furred creatures peek and pry,
Frisk under the boughs and out,
For every one of the wood folk knows
What the wood is whispering about.

But ever when winter's noon draws near
And the blinding storms slant down,
When the buck and the doe fleet over the snow
And the choppers come out from the town;

Then keenly, keenly the axes ring
Where the snow drifts curl and press,
For the choppers have chosen the straightest firs
Of a tall man's height or less.

And down in the village homes by night
You can hear the children shout
When the candles alight on the Christmas trees
Through the dim, wet panes shine out.

There are gay little gifts on the silvery twigs,
And candles on every bough,
And the fir tree trembles its fibers through
For we know its secret now.

*

For we hear in a tale of the cross and the star
That brighten the long time through,
And the gift that came to the world with these,—
The Christmas tale that is true.

And we love to think that the silver fir
In the shape of a star is set
And the young green twigs into crosses grow
That men may never forget,

When the Christmas lights burn low, burn low,
And the year is past its tide,
When the children gather their gifts in sleep,
And the tree is cast aside.

But the hills that slope to the curdled streams
Feel never a lack nor a loss,
For others will grow in the sleet and the snow
In the shape of the star and the cross.

O the wind it wends through the young green leaves,
And a whisper runs in the wood,
For the kind earth worketh her will in them,
And the will of the earth is good.

Sailor Dead—Soldier Dead

Soldier dead, soldier dead,
Do you wake and know the hour
When the children two and two—
Rosy flag and rosy flower—
Stir the grave grass with their marching overhead?
Do you quicken to no sigh,
Does no smallest piercing cry
Break the silence where you lie,
Soldier dead?

Once we left our books and play,
Once we came with running feet,
When we heard the stirring drum,
Heard the soldiers in the street,
When we pushed between the knees along the line,
When we saw the jackets blue,
Heard the fifer fifing true,
Then we wished that we were you,
Brave and fine.

Now we think how still you lie,
And how low your grassy tents,
Think how chill the graveyard air,
And how cold the monuments;
So we know you must be glad to have us come,
Glad of blossoms that we spill,
Glad of banners bright and still,
Of the fifer fifing shrill,
And the drum.

Sailor dead, sailor dead,
From the pastures that you knew,

Where the upland plover pipes,
From the woodlands where they grew,
Here are garlands we have gathered, white and red,
And we cast them on the waves
From the shore your valor saves,
For we do not know your graves,
Sailor dead.

Sailor dead, soldier dead,
Though our thoughts are little worth,
Yet our thinking comes to this,
Only you of all the earth
Know the wonder that is hid from such as we,
Why we draw the quickened breath,
Why we pant for soldier death
When the trumpet cries and saith,
'Follow me!'

Now the files of veterans go,
Now the crowds and music pass,
Will you whisper to us true,
Whisper through the leaning grass,—
As we spell among the graves the thing you know?
What we pant for you have found,
Lying straightly under ground,
Without motion, without sound,
All a-row.

But we cannot hear it plain
For the trumpet frets and cries,
And we cannot see it clear
For the banners blind our eyes,
And the warm air stirs the bright boughs overhead,
And we think perhaps we, too,

Must come here to lie with you
Ere we get the message true,
Soldier dead.

Thanksgiving

When we sit down to turkey, roast turkey,
—A plump and crispy drumstick or a tender slice of breast—
When we sit down to turkey on a Thursday in November
To cranberries and celery and gravy and the rest;
With second helps of everything so savory and hot,
When we sit down to turkey there's something to remember,
And someone to be thankful to that's usually forgot.

When we sit down to pumpkin pie and maple syrup sundae,
To potatoes and tomatoes and to luscious lima beans,
To succotash and peanuts and clams and popping corn,
There's something to be thought besides what Thanksgiving
    means—
And Puritans and Presidents to whom our thanks are due,—
About a thousand years before a Puritan was born,
Among the first Americans who gave these things to you.

There's something to be thought of with gratitude and wonder
On the grass called *teosinte* which the patient Redman found,
Which he loved and labored over till it answered with a yield
That has saved a world from famine; and the tuber small
    and round
Which he coaxed to be potatoes, and the seed whose snowy fleece
Makes the half of all our clothing, and the smoke that going round
In after dinner comfort, spells a full-fed people's peace.

When we sit down to turkey, roast turkey,
There are thanks too long ungiven, and things that must
    be thought
About the first Americans whom so seldom we remember,
And whether we've repaid them for the things they gave and
    taught,
And if not, is there something we could do to make amends,

When we sit down to turkey on a Thursday in November
On a day that all Americans should be the best of friends.

Editor's Notes

Teosinte is "an annual grass of Central America . . . now widely cultivated as a valuable fodder plant, sometimes also as a cereal" (*Oxford English Dictionary*).

Songs the Indians Sing

Rain Song of the Rio Grande Pueblos

People of the Middle Heaven
Come to us, come to us!
People of the rainbow,
COME, COME, COME, COME,
People of the thunder,
COME . . . O COME!
People of the lightning,
Send your serpent darting arrows!
COME, COME, COME, COME,
People of the white clouds,
White blossom clouds of the Middle Heaven Meadows
Come to us, come to us!
People of the dark clouds,
COME, COME, COME, COME,
Level lying clouds of the straight stretched mesas
Moving to and fro, to make the earth more fruitful
Pour down, pour down
RAIN, RAIN, RAIN!

Editor's Notes

Compare "Rain Songs for the Rio Grande Pueblos" in *American Rhythm* (1923).

Austin's note: "This is one of many songs sung by the Pueblo Indians in New Mexico to bring rain. It is a dance song, and should be sung to the rhythm of the big drum saying, Come, Come, Come, Come, without any accent."

Song of Life Renewal

The wind stirs the willows,
The wind stirs the grasses!

The cottonwoods are growing tall
They are growing tall and green.

From the Paiute.

Editor's Notes

Austin's note: "This song was sung by Paiutes at the Ghost Dance many years ago when they were expecting the buffalo to come back and bring the great day of the Indians again."

The Road-Runner

Road-Runner with the crested head
Goes crying poi, poi,
As he runs around the house,
Poi, poi, all around the house.

Here is the lonely road-runner
Poi, poi, the lonely road-runner,
He eats lizards in the morning,
He eats solitary lizards.

Here is the red-eyed road-runner,
Poi, poi, the red-eyed road-runner
Who runs about the mistletoe,
This is the red-eyed road-runner.

I run and hide
I run and hide,
Now I kill gray lizard,
His fat body I eat up.
        I run and hide,
        I run and hide
        In the garramboya bush.

From the Pima.

Editor's Notes

Austin's note: "This is a Pima song collected by Frank Russel; it is about a bird, known as 'Chaparral Cock,' or, in Spanish, 'Corridor del Camino,' which is the same as road-runner, very well known in the desert parts of the Southwest." The Pima are also known as Akimel O'odham, the River People, and are closely associated with the Tohono O'odham. Traditionally they lived on the Gila River and the Salt River in southern Arizona.

Chicken-Hawk's Song

That old owl there,
He hates me, he hates me,
That old owl,
Because I bring home rabbits,
White tailed rabbits,
Tender, flopping rabbits,
When he brings none!

From the Navajo.

Editor's Notes

Austin's source for this poem and "Glossy Locks" is Washington Matthews, "Navajo Gambling Songs," *American Anthropologist* 2 (January 1889): 1–19; rpt. Washington, D.C.: Judd & Detweiler, 1889.

Glossy Locks

Glossy Locks picks them up,
Glossy Locks picks them up,
Little Dove picks them up,
The lucky ones,
The winning ones.
    Ai, Little Dove!

Red Moccasin picks them up,
Red Moccasin picks them up,
Little Dove picks them up,
He picks them for me
The lucky ones,
    For me, Little Dove!

From the Navajo.

Editor's Notes

Austin's note: "These are two Navajo gambling songs sung while the dice are being thrown. 'Glossy Locks' and 'Red Moccasin' refer to the glossy plumage and red feet of the dove."

Buffalo Songs

Behold me, I arise,
Mon-non-ti-de, I arise
The great chief buffalo
Whose tread makes the earth rumble.
I arise, Hiu-gthe-ton-ga,
In whose thighs there is strength,
I arise now,
I who am called Tail-curved-back
In my anger, I arise.

Behold me, I arise,
The bull buffalo,
In whose humped shoulders there is power,
I arise, Pa-he-ga-sho,
I who shakes his mane, raging,
When I am brought to bay.
I arise now.

Behold me, I arise,
Curved-horns, He-thi-sdu-sha,
They are very sharp,
With them I make knife wounds,
With them I prevail against the foe.
Behold me, I who obey the Mysterious One,
Commanded to go forth
Into the visible world,
I the great bull buffalo,
I arise!

From the Osage.

Fire Drill Songs

I

Kindle, kindle ye the fire!

Twirl, twirl, twirl the fire drill,
Twirl the spindle and the bow,
Twirl and grind!

Twirl the fire sticks,
Twirl till they sing.
Twirl till the sparks come,
Kindle, kindle ye the flame!

Twirl, twirl, till the smoke comes,
A blue thread, the smoke comes,
Twirl till the flames rise,
The red flames rise.
Twirl and grind!

II

Look you!
I make the fire,
Red fire I make,
Watch the flames as they rise.

Look you!
I make the fire,
The flames stand upright.
The fire I am making!

Look you!
With the fire sticks,

With the spindle and the bow
I the fire make.
I drop it on the tinder,
See the flames spread.
Lo, the fire is made!

From the Osage.

Corn-Planting Songs

(Sung by Osage women as they press the corn seed into the ground with their feet)

I

Footprints I have made,
Sacred footprints,
Over the corn hill.
Footprints I have made,
They lie in even lines
Firming the planted seed.

Footprints I have made,
Mysterious footprints,
They are broken now
By the small green spears,
Footprints through which come up
Green leafy stalks of the corn.
They wave to each other in the wind.
Footprints I have made,
Over them the young corn ears
Lean to each other in profusion,
Over the footprints I have made
I pluck the foodful ears,
The ripe corn I gather.

II

My footprints, that lie in even lines,
Over them I break the dry stalks,
Gray litter of stalks covers the ground,
From my house gray smoke arises,

There is joy in my house
Because of the abundant corn.

My footprints!
The footprints I have made
They are sacred and mysterious,
Through them life has come,
Life of the corn which is my life,
Through my footprints!

III

The footprints I have made,
I shall go to see them!
The footprints that lie in even rows.
I shall go to see
The earth broken through the footprints,
The stalks that stand with spreading blades,
The broad blades waving in the wind
I shall go to see.

I shall go to see
The ears that overhang and cross each other,
The ripe ears I shall gather.

I shall go to see
The pale broken ends of stalks
Like blossoms over the field,
I shall go to see the ripened ears
That cause smoke to rise in my house,
That bring joy to my house
The joy of fruition,
The day of harvest!

From the Osage.

Editor's Notes

Austin notes that "Buffalo Songs," "Fire Drill Songs," and "Corn Planting Songs" were "first collected by Francis La Flesche, an Omaha Indian who works for the Smithsonian Institution." For "Corn Planting Songs," see *The 36th Annual Report of the Bureau of Ethnology, 1914–1915* (Washington, D.C.: Government Printing Office, 1921), 295–96. La Flesche's work on the Osage and other Omaha tribes is useful for developing a sense of the importance of the buffalo, the sacred fireplaces, and corn in the social life and rituals. See Alice Fletcher and Francis La Flesche, "The Omaha Tribe," *The 27th Annual Report of the Bureau of American Ethnology, 1905-1906* (Washington, D.C.: Government Printing Office, 1911). Rpt. 2 volumes, Lincoln: University of Nebraska Press, 1972.

Mountain Chant

I

The voice that beautifies the land,
The voice above!
The voice of the thunder
Within the dark cloud.
Again and again it sounds,
Thonah, thonah,
The voice of the thunder!

The voice that beautifies the land,
The voice below!
The voice of the grasshopper,
Among the plants,
Again and again it sounds,
The voice that beautifies the land.

II

In beauty may I walk
All day long may I walk
Through the returning season may I walk
On the trail marked with pollen may I walk
With grasshoppers about my feet may I walk
With dew about my feet may I walk
With beauty before me may I walk
With beauty behind me may I walk
With beauty above me may I walk
With beauty below me may I walk
In old age wandering on a trail of beauty may I walk
Lively may I walk
In old age wandering, living again,

In beauty may I walk.
In beauty it is finished!

III

In the house of dawn,
In the house made of evening twilight,
In the house made of dark cloud,
The path to which is on the rainbow
Where the zigzag lightning stands high on top.
Oh, rain god,
With your moccasins of dark cloud, come to us,
With the rainbow hanging high on the ends of your wings
Come to us soaring!

From the Navajo.

Editor's Notes

Austin uses Navajo translations from Washington Matthews, perhaps by way of Nellie Barnes's *American Indian Love Lyrics and Other Verse* (New York: Macmillan, 1925). The source is Matthews, "Navaho Myths, Prayers, and Songs," *American Archaeology and Ethnology* 5, no. 2 (September 1907): 21–63. Austin wrote a foreword to the Barnes anthology and contributed some texts from *American Rhythm* (1923), as well as supporting Barnes's analysis of Indian poetics.

Austin's note: "This is a Navajo medicine dance given to secure good health, and these are parts of the songs that are sung on that occasion. The refrains are repeated four times because the Navajos regard four as a lucky number."

MAGAZINE AND PERIODICAL PUBLICATIONS

The thirty-five poems collected here, arranged chronologically by date of publication, give a wide range of Mary Austin's poetry, dating from one of her first magazine publications in April 1899 to two of her last in 1932. The range of magazines is also impressive. Austin began by publishing in *St. Nicholas* magazine, a journal aimed at children and adolescent readers, and she broke into adult print with Charles Lummis's *Land of Sunshine* and *Out West*, both published in Los Angeles, and the *Overland Monthly*, published in San Francisco. From those beginnings, Austin soon found her way to such large-circulation periodicals as *Cosmopolitan*, *McClure's*, and the *New York Independent*. Her publications in such prestigious literary and cultural journals as *Poetry*, the *Nation*, *Harper's*, *Atlantic Monthly*, and the *Saturday Review of Literature* solidified her reputation as a practicing poet in the first quarter of the twentieth century.

The poems may seem less characteristic of Austin's best work than those collected in *The American Rhythm* (1923) and *The Children Sing in the Far West* (1928). They are certainly more discursive, verging on chattiness on occasion. But in certain texts, such as "Home Thoughts in the City" and "Mountain Parable," we see Austin writing some of her best free-verse poems about the Southwest and its powerful landscapes.

Little Light Moccasin

Little Light Moccasin swings in her basket,
Woven of willow and sinew of deer,
Nursed by the pine tree and rocked by the breezes,
Wonderful things are to see and to hear.

Wide is the sky from the top of the mountain,
Sheltered the cañon from glare of the sun,
Ere she is wearied of watching their changes,
Little Light Moccasin finds she can run.

Brown is her skin as the bark of the birches,
Light are her feet as the feet of the fawn,
Shy little daughter of mesa and mountain,
Little Light Moccasin wakes with the dawn.

All of the treasures of summertime cañons,
These are the playthings the little maid knows,
Berry time, blossom time, bird calls and butterflies,
Columbine trumpet and sweet brier rose.

Bear meat and deer meat, with pine nuts and acorns,
Handfuls of honeycomb dripping with sweet,
Taboose of joint grass the meadows provide her,
Bulbs of wild hyacinth, pleasant to eat.

When on the mesa the meadow lark stooping
Folds his barred wings on the low hidden nest,
Called by the condor and hushed by the elf owl,
Little Light Moccasin goes to her rest.

Counting the stars through the chinks of the wickiup,
Watching the flames on its leafy walls leap,

Hearing the song of the wind in the pine trees,
Little Light Moccasin falls fast asleep.

Editor's Notes

Land of Sunshine, April 1899, 261.

Inyo

Far from the northward, from the cloven ridges
Pine-girt, deep-drifted with bewildering snows,
Through ice-plowed gorge, the leaping river bridges,
Light span by span, from lake to lake below;
Through mountain meadow and the snow-fed hollow
Where birch and buckthorn thickets mark the trail,
Spurning the tawny hills in haste to follow
The long brown reaches of a desert vale.

To east and west roll up the purple ranges
Foot bound about with leopard-colored hills,
From east to west their serrate shadow changes,
From east and west stream down the tumbling rills
That mock the shadeless slopes and sullen ledges;
Through sunburnt wastes of sage and yellow sand,
Flow down to meet thy willows and thy sedges,
O lonely river, in a lonely land!

Foamless and swift thy winding waters follow
To find, unbosomed to the wind-swept skies,
The great lake lapping in a tideless hollow,
Wanton to each day's changes as they rise;
Purpling to meet the splendor of the mornings,
Paling to catch their tender mid-day blue,
Trembling alike to smilings and to scornings,
Fleet light of loves, it cannot hold one true.

Like some great lioness beside the river
With furies flaming in her half-shut eyes,
Watching the light from heated sands up-quiver—
Untamed and barren, lone the valley lies.
Forego, O River, all the wrong you do her,
Hasting thy waters to the bitter lake,

Rise from thy reedy marges and subdue her!
So shall the land be fertile for thy sake.

Editor's Notes

Overland Monthly, July 1899, 49.

"Inyo" is the country of the Owens Valley, the Alabama Hills, and the eastern slope of the Sierra Nevadas.

The Feet of the Young Men

Acts V., 9.

Where the nations sat in council, scarlet robe and purple hem,
From the four-went ways of travel came the poor of God to them;
Came the blind of right and reason, came the halt of rule and law,
Came the feeble, feckless peoples, crying dole of all they saw.

> "Lo, to you God giveth bread,
> Break a crust to us," they said,
> "We have eaten fruit of bondage to the core;"
> "Take, and eat," the nations cried,
> Here is freedom;" but they lied,
> *And the young men's feet were at the door.*

"All we know of truth to Godward, all we can of love beside,
All our good sword arm hath won us," quoth the nations; but they
lied,
Bid them wait upon the scarlet, puppet to the purple hem—
As they dealt with hungry peoples, so the Lord hath dealt with them.

> They have felt the threshing flail,
> They have passed beyond the pale,
> To the limbo of lost empires gone before,
> They are stricken in their pride,
> They are dead, because they lied—
> *And the young men's feet are at the door.*

Though your word shall run with power, and your arm reach
overseas,
Yet the questing bolt shall find you if you keep not faith with these,
Lest you be at one with Egypt, lest you lie as Rome lies now
In the potter's field of empires, mint and cumin, keep the vow.

*

Keep the truth your fathers made
Lest your children grow afraid,
Lest you hear the captives' mothers weeping sore—
There is little worth beside—
They are dead because they lied,
And the young men's feet are at the door.

Editor's Notes

Land of Sunshine, February 1900, 139.

The Gods of the Saxon

We have set the white Christ forward, we have bid the old gods go,
We be Christians, Christian peoples, singing psalm tunes staid
and slow.
We have strewn the graven idols, we are bounden to the Lord,
In hoc signo it is written—but we prove it with the sword.

For the old gods played us hazards, and they tracked us in
their wrath
By the smoke of sacrifices that we made along our path;
Saved us to outwit each other; broke us if they listed then,
And at best of all their saving they were gods and we were men.

But the White Christ he is lowly, he hath thorns about his brow,
He hath sorrowed, he hath suffered,—Lord what boots thy sorrow
now?
Seeing that we give our brother to the kite-kind and the crow,
And the shell-strewn bones to whiten where the shy wild cattle go.

And the old gods gather, gather, where the shrilling bugles break,
For the hot blown breath of battle fans the elder gods awake,
Calling high above the trumpets, saying, "Thus the old rune runs,
By the net that took the fathers ye shall surely snare the sons.

"By the bitter lust of empire, by the fret of boasts withstood,
By the itch of prideful peoples that must make their boastings good,
In the fern damp, by the velt-side, we have brought them stark
and low,
They that wake no more for mornings, nor for any winds that
blow."

We be Christians, Christian peoples, thinking scorn of ruder days,
But above the *Pax Vobiscum*, keener than the prayers we raise,
Come the jeering gods of warfare from the ends of all the earth,

By the White Christ, wan and wounded, and they mock him
with their mirth.

Editor's Notes

AU 208; published in the *New York Independent*, April 26, 1900, 996.

The poem seems to refer to the British involvement in southern Africa, leading to the Second Boer War (1899–1902). See also the poem "The Burgher's Wife" in this section.

A Twilight Hill

A grove I know, set circling like a crown,
Of slanting oaks; it overlooks a town,
And thence the hill front slopeth broadly down
        And gives a prospect fair.
When days of spring draw lengthening to a close,
The while from room to room the housewife goes
With busy cares about the night's repose,
        I love to linger there.

It is the season when the waters sing,
Green, misty censers do the grape vines swing,
And at their thresholds birds are gossiping
        While holds the lengthening light.
And here the blundering night-moth doth disclose
The scented hollow where the currant grows,
And there the musky bloom of gilia glows
        Like nuns at prayer, milk-white.

Some beams still light the far, dark, tapered firs,
A quail belated to its covert whirrs
In nestling hollows where a warm wind stirs
        The lupines everywhere.
The hill folk have no fear of such as I.
Thc qucsting night hawk hurtlcs dauntlcss by,
I hear the specked owlets hoot, and spy
        Their matings unaware.

While lowing upward from the winding creek
The warm, last-lighted slopes the cattle seek,
Up climbs the dark along the jacinth steep,
        And every far hill glows
Blue with the blue of seas encompassing,
Divinely purpled to its outer ring,

In such uncounted hours remembering
    The sea from which it rose.

Editor's Notes

Land of Sunshine, March 1901, 181.

Austin's manuscript note locates the hill above the arroyo between Los Angeles and Pasadena.

The Burgher's Wife [In the British Detention Camp]

Outside the guard goes heavily; the sun beats on the roof;
He hears the sick ones moaning, but he holds his eyes aloof.
In heaven is only sun glare, dust devils on the veldt;
We could not pray the clouds up, however long we knelt.
There are women who are sullen, there are women who are
wild,
And one perhaps is hopeful, but that one has no child;
Katrina raved when yesternoon they took her last away;
Annetje's went at candle light, and mine will go today.

And is it you, brave England, that holds us in the pen,
Making war on wives and children since you cannot match
our men?
Will you swallow up our nation, make our name as
naught, you think?
By the living God of Dutchmen, you shall spew the broth
you drink!

I had seven sons, how long ago! Seven and my good man,
And Greta—only woman child that came to me and Jan—
Six strong sons of my body and one that still was small;
They were stout for war or praying, and their country
took them all—
The wolf, the kite, the river trench, by kopje and by veldt.
I did not keep, though all their wounds I in my body felt;
It was I that scoured their rifles—one had hardly done
with play—
I did not weep to see them go, but I shall weep today.

And is it wise, great England, to build your greatness so—
You that fatten on small peoples, though, God's faith,
the meal is slow?
Growing wider by the holdings of a simpler, feebler folk,

It is fatness where no strength is, and you, too, shall feel
the yoke.

But once I wept for Wilhelm—he had his father's looks;
The day that he was turned sixteen he put away his books.
"Now kiss me mother, let me go, for I am grown a man."
And so I wept for Wilhelm, though I did not weep for Jan.
And for myself no whimper; I am past my bearing time,
But I wept to know my woman child must die before her
prime.
Is no coolness on the pillow for the tender, fevered head?
Is no comfort in the sickness but my tear and captive's bread?

It is not for you, O England, to give me back my sons;
We have paid the tale twice over by the coughing, spitting
guns,
But the small graves of children, they are yawning in the sod,
Deep enough to gulf your glory, high to witness unto God.

Editor's Notes

Land of Sunshine, December 1901, 423–24.

The Second Boer War (1899–1902) led to the British victory over Dutch settlers and eventually to the foundation of the Union of South Africa.

A Pipe of Oaten Straw

When south winds smelt of earth and brooks ran clear
I made a little pipe of oaten straw;
From such of old the shepherd lads could draw,
Each on the green sward laid, his love anear,
Such strains as voiced the blithe, young-hearted year,
Till down the greenwood aisles the piper saw
Small, shy, wood creatures hushed of wing and paw,
All wrapt and still to give his piping ear.

Perchance he'd heard Pan pipe the reeds among,
Or his blown breath along the fluted pines,
Or lilting choruses by gleaners sung
Wine-red and merry in the Tuscan vines,
Or Satyr's lyre that charmed a shy wood-maid,
And mixed their music with the airs he played.

Perhaps no loftier strains the shepherd knew
Than pee-whits calling the young world awake,
Or tranquil music such as hylas make
When jewel weeds drip all with starry dew,
Or cry of weanling lamb and travailing ewe,
Or rattling reeds that in the wind do quake,
Or wild, untutored melodies that brake
Across the piper's fancy while he blew.

But thin as summer rill the music flowed,
Not over loud, but sweet and crystal clear,
And all his thought unto his true-love showed.
Ah, if a listening heart down bent to hear
Such skill were mine, compelling notes to draw
Form this, my little pipe of oaten straw.

Editor's Notes

Cosmopolitan, May 1902, 79.

The Young Leader

God said, "Although the land is young
        My people have grown weary-wise,
To wag the smooth, excusing tongue
        And watch with easy, tolerant eyes.
Although," He said, "the land is strong
        And not yet come to her full prime,
My people jostle cheeks with wrong
        They might have conquered in good time.

"Less careful of the goal they grow
        Observing those who walk beside,
To line up smoothly they forego
        The purchase of the younger stride.
Too wise they grow for hero work;
        And prideful sophistries of ease
That else they trampled in the murk,
        Now swathe like weeds about their knees.

"One need I in this strong young land
        Whose heart shall with the land's heart beat,
To give my people to his hand
        And time their marching to his feet.
They lag before their work is done
        Like over-fed and aging men,
Now will I find them such an one
        To make the pace for them again."

And so God set the cunning gin
        Of place and hour and human stress
To let the younger leaven in
        To work His will out in the press.
Not as men choose, but as God sends—
We have no right of pride in this—

Since one such sending makes amends
For many choosings gone amiss.

Editor's Notes

Out West, July 1902, 68.

The Song of the Bow

Red Morning came to the evergreen oak
        And wove him a screen of boughs,
To lie in wait till the tall dun buck
Came over the hill to browse.

It was all in the time of tender leaves
        And the blossoming hour of the vine,
The red fox barked in the cactus scrub
        And he heard the wild bees whine.

It was all in the time of tender leaves
        And poppies beginning to blow;
Red Morning sat in the evergreen oak
        And made him a song of his bow.

The wood was the heart of a juniper tree
        On a strong, sea-sloping hill,
And the thing it learned in the young green bough
        The bow remembered still;

For it learned of the wind, it learned of the sea
        And it learned of the spotted snake,
And their threefold sting was loosed from the string
        When the will of the bow would wake.

The cord of the bow is the will of the bow,
        'Tis the twisted gut of the deer;
Red Morning fingered the feathered shaft
        And drew the butt to his ear.

For he was aware of an antlered buck
        Come down by the stream to feed;

Red Morning loosened the cord of the bow
        And sent him the stinging reed.

And all by night when the braves came in
        And the children lay in the byre,
Red Morning sang his song of the bow
        As he leaped by the leaping fire.

But the tall buck ranged on the hill no more
        Nor belled to the tender doe,
For never a beast runs free in the wood
        Who has harked to the song of the bow.

Editor's Notes

Out West, January 1904, 55.

Night Wind, Wake!

Night Wind wake! now the cattle leave the trail for us,
Huddled on the hill slope by the stony water-scar,
        Get you down along the steep
        Where the moon-eyed gilias keep,
        To go walking in the meadows—
        Silver runnels in the meadows—
Where the blossoms star the shadows and the hidden waters are.

Night Wind wake! now the laden vine is calling us,
Calling with the incense of its green and misty blooms,
        Now the milk-white alders quake
        Where the dark lies like a lake
        On the musky scented meadows,
        On the many-lilied meadows,
On the chilly mountain meadows where the throaty hyla booms.

Night Wind wake! I am coming up the trail to you,
Up and past the gullies where the midnight shadows lair
        Past the tangle by the creek
        Where the trail is all to seek,
        To the damp and dusky meadows,
        To the willow-skirted meadows,
To go walking in the meadows with the pleasant Night Wind there.

Editor's Notes

Out West, April 1904, 318.

The magazine misprints "blooms" for "booms," which Austin corrected in her copy. *Gilia* is a diverse genus in the phlox family; the *hyla* is a vocal tree frog.

A Pioneer

Goodhope came out of Warwick Mead
Hating the law of the elder son,
And the old world rule by which they breed
Each to the guerdon his father won.
Never a chance for God to make
Good true men for their manhood's sake.

Goodhope came to a big new land,
Noblest ever a true man trod,
Hollow and hillslope fitly planned
Fresh from the glacier mills of God:
Rain wet steeps where the redwoods grew,
Rivers roaring the valleys through.

That was a land for a man to love,—
Rosy the snow the dun cloud spills
Over the dark, spiked pines above,
Rosy with blossom the round browed hills,
Wind sown lichens of russet and red,
Never a rock uncomforted.

Goodhope gave of his best to the land,
For a new land asks of a man his best,
Blood, and body, and brains and hand,
Goodhope trusted the land for the rest.
And the land repaid him the deep drawn breath,
And high red pulse that laughs at death.

Paid him the increase of barn and byre,
Drudged for him deep in her secret ways,
Wrought him a balm for his heart's desire,
Rendered him coin of her noble days;

Mothered him, moulded him ’til he grew
Fittest for working her purpose through.

Goodhope wrestled with flood and wood,
And this is the law of the pioneer,
Where one true man makes a footing good
Ten true fellows may stand next year.
Into the wilderness drove the wedge,
Men like these were its cutting edge.

Goodhope walked in a fair large town—
Mill smoke wreathing the thin white spires,
Whispers of empire ran up and down
Pulsing over the world strung wires,—
Heard men say with a laugh and a sneer,
“There is old Goodhope, the pioneer.”

Goodhope died at the end of days,
Men with their feet in the ruts of trade
Dealt him a tardy dole of praise
For the good they won from the chance he made.
Said, It is well that our schemes have room;
Elbowed and jostled above his tomb.

Raised to him never a monument,
Left him prone in his well loved sod.
Back to its blossoms his ashes went,
But somewhere far in the hills of God,
Farther than prophet or sage can peer,
The spirit of Goodhope is pioneer.

Editor’s Notes

New York Independent, January 3, 1907, 40.

The Covenant

This poem was written on the day the good news came from California and read for the first time by the author at the jubilee meeting at Cooper Union in New York.

Long have we looked for a sign, my land, that we are thy
daughters indeed,
Who are not born of the blood, but yet at thy knee were nursed,
Who are only foster kin to that stalwart, strenuous breed
Who of the men of all lands shall yet be called finest and first;
Mother of mountains, thou who has mothered us at our need,
Now is the covenant sealed that we are thy daughters indeed.

Gladly we sprang to thy call from the world-rims east and south,
Loving and working thy will from the coastwise hills to the sea,
Loving the light of thy skies and the kiss of thy golden mouth—
But long in despite of our loving you pushed us off from your knee,
Denied us the wages we won in the sun and the sand and the
drought,
Wrong didst thou then to thy daughters, wrong, O land of the West
and South.

But now you remit us the work of our hands, and the free
untrammeled stride
Neck and neck with the men we bore. Was the seed of the fruit
more worth
Than the willing flesh which wrapped it soft, that we walked
not side by side?
Could we have been feeble and fool at once, and not stamped them
at the birth
With the stripe that all men point to and all they decry and deride?
Can you trail the bearing bough in the dust, and the fruit keep
high in its pride?

*

This is the guerdon we won in the earthquake shock and the fire,
When the rip of the flames was hid where the sea wind warred
with the smoke,
When you wrenched at the rooted rocks, when you kindled at
cornice and spire.
O, nurse of the strong man-strain, did we whimper or cry at
the stroke?
When the gutted street was foul and sick in the slot of the
racing fire,
Did you hear us laugh as we fought and ran? And now you
have paid us our hire!

You have shaped us large to adventure, O land new-tamed, elate,
Now we shall work our endeavor out, we have leave to choose
and prefer;
And the sign of your larger sovereignty, O Mistress of the Gate,
Is the work we shall do in our city who have built our blood in her.
You had shamed our pride by your ghost-grey seas round which
the ranked hills wait,
Had you lost us step with the strong young lands who herald the
coming State.

Long shall the covenant run, my land, to the sons of our sons begot,
Who have felt thy pulse in the dark and drawn thee in at the breast,
(Beautiful, bounteous, keen, desolate, waste and hot
All that thou art and hast, known and approved of the best).
This is the sword in our hand, to fight for thy ultimate need;
This is the seal you have set, that we are thy daughters indeed!

Editor's Notes

Woman's Journal, October 21, 1911, 336.

The magazine was, according to its masthead, the "official organ of the National American Woman Suffrage Association." The

Woman's Journal of a week earlier noted that California had voted for equal suffrage, becoming the sixth state to do so after Wyoming, Colorado, Utah, Idaho, and Washington. Austin joined a celebration, reading her poem to an exuberant crowd.

The Song of the Hills

Being the Song of a Man and a Woman
Who Might Have Loved
(From the Yokut)

This is the song of the Hills
In the hour when they talk together,
When the alpen glow dies down in the west and leaves
the heavens tender;
In the pure and shadowless hour
When the Mountains talk together;

"Fir tree leaneth to fir,
The wind-blown willows mingle;
Clouds draw each to each, dissolve, depart, and renew
one another;
But the strong Hills hold asunder.

"Had we been less we had loved;
We had stooped and been tender;

"But our hands are under the earth
For the travail of her harvests,
Upholding the rain-sleeked fields
And the long, brown, fruitful furrow.
Terror taketh the earth
When the Mountains move together.

"But ever as winds of Spring
Set the meadow grasses caressing,
And the coo-dove's call
To the coo-dove's mate
Resounds in the oak-wood valleys,
We shall thrill with the brooding earth,

We shall turn, touch hands, and remember,
Had we been less, how much we had loved,
How nobly we might have been tender."

Editor's Notes

McClure's, October 1911, 615; reprinted in *Path on the Rainbow*, 218–19.

The Peace Prospect
(As distinguished by the ordinary person)

Our vicar he preaches of peace upon earth,
All embracing, enduring, unbroken;
It is two thousand years since that message had birth,
And—what do you think of the token?

Goes shrilling the fife and the drum;
Ah, quick, how the maids are a-flutter,
And the children will trail in the wake of the guns,
And the gamins will cheer from the gutter.
(Time was when they fought from the gutter.)
Pipe up to the tune of a march,
Barbaric, staccato and stirring,
Set some small bits of rag
To the fore for a flag,
Red and white are the hues for preferring;
There is that in your breast bids it swell with the rest,
Sets the blood in your pulses a-whirring.

The smoke curls as high as the spire,
Hammer and drill they roar under,
And the red flames that lick at the sweat of the men
Forging the engines of thunder,
(And death will walk forth in the thunder.)
And men will go down in the lees of the sea,
Darkling go groping and peering,
Go setting them mines
To be sprung in the times
When the ships of our foes shall be nearing,
When they roll in their pride on the comb of the tide,
Hostile and keen and unfearing.

*

The peoples they snarl and bare teeth,
        Making boasts for their children's long ruling,
And the heathen that live over seas—
        Good Lord, what the heathen are doing!
        (Time comes they shall sweat for that doing.)
Our gods and the goods that we make—
He must swallow the one with the other—
The truths we have won
At the point of the gun
We will take over seas to our brother,
And the guns make it plain that our good is his gain,
        (And Sundays we still call him brother.)

Oh, the vicar no doubt has the right to the fore,
        And, besides, he is paid for his preaching,
But a new Maxim gun with a very large bore
        Would mightily help at the teaching.
When we've shown him the rule of our thumb,
        When the gods at his gates have been broken,
In time we may loosen the snares of our drum,
        But—what do you think of the token?

Editor's Notes

The source is a newspaper clipping with "Independence, Cal." at the bottom with Austin's name; the typescript in *AU* 439 clarifies the text and notes that the poem was "published in San Francisco Chronicle," but without date.

San Jacinto

Westward the mesa
Squares seaward like an altar,
Lit by the wax white yucca candles.

White undersides of lilac leaves
Riffle in the sea wind,
Breaking in blue smoke of blossoms,
Blue as incense and fresher,
Thick stems of manzanita and mahogany
Twine like carved choir stalls.

There sits the maiden thrush,
There the treble of the cañon wren
Drips like cool water out of sight.

Was that the wind that stirred
The antlered chaparral,
Or blacktail, nose to flank
Slipping delicately?
Did grey sisters glide
To the organ loft,
Or did the dun sides of mule deer
Bound up the rocky stairs of San Jacinto?

Far down the nave, the sea
Murmurs its immemorial responses,
White panicles of greasewood bow and lift
Like ladies at their prayers,
And where their green mantillas part
Run lines of yellow violets
Like golden rosaries
Broken and scattered in the grass.

*

Outside, against thick yellow sands
The spangled ice plant spreads
A rosy web, beyond it blue of the beach lupines,
Then the orange streak
Of dormidera dims the mustard gold.
That was old Spain, I think,
Who passed this way,
And like a careless dancer left
Her scarf along the shore.

Editor's Notes

El Palacio, March 1919, 93.

Mount San Jacinto rises in the San Jacinto Mountain Range, Riverside County, California.

The Singing Dunes of Ensenada Todos Santos

Behind there is a ring of pointed hills,
New hills not yet worn down
To the soothed contours of old age.
Red hills stippled in dull green,
Pale hills spotted like an ocelot,
Pricked with cactus, thorn and flame.

Outside, the bay
Catches and cradles all the blue
Of South Pacific swells,
Playing with it as a child
Plays with its mother's jewels;
Huddled in the hollow of a wave
Or tossed on white foam fingers,
Touched with amber fire along its edges.
Suddenly the wind
Snatches the sapphire to its far horizon.
The bay, slapped pale and bereft,
Runs whimpering up the beaches.
Between the hills and the bay
The dunes shape and reshape,
Docile as a dog or a woman.
Sharp sided sands,
White as the moon at midday,
Run up, hill pointed, in the land wind,
Run down, wave curved, in the sea gusts.

Here and there yellow and lilac
Umbels of the sea verbena
Hold for a season the shape of a hill or a billow,
Spreading a delicate, sickly scent,
The regrets of a fond inconsistence.

*

The unceasing movement
Of sharp sided particles, one upon the other,
Gives forth a tone, wind like
But with the crystal tang of musical glasses.
It is the heart of the dunes
Singing as it remembers
First the land from which it was torn,
Next, the sea that claimed it.

Oh, singing dunes of Ensenada Todos Santos,
Even so I am shifted and shaped
Between the Earth and the Earth-Encompassing,
Even so do I give forth
The strident, musical note of my indecisions.

Editor's Notes

El Palacio, March 1919, 93.

Ensenada de Todos Santos is the former name for the Mexican town of Ensenada in northern Baja California, situated on the Todos Santos Bay and now a popular beach resort.

San Juan Love Song

When first I saw my maiden,
When first my eyes beheld her,
All amid the corn

Like butterflies about my heart
Her looks came glancing,
Like butterflies amid the corn
My heart was dancing
When first I saw my maiden,
When first my eyes beheld her,
All amid the corn
Blue butterflies were dancing.

Editor's Notes

Harper's Magazine, June 1921, 78.

Of a group of six poems in *Harper's*, this is the only one not republished in *The American Rhythm* (1923). The others are "Woman's Song," "Rain Songs from the Rio Grande Pueblos," "Lament of a Man for his Son," "Songs of the Friend," and "Song for the Newborn." San Juan is a pueblo near Santa Fe, New Mexico.

Drouth

I

What way shall a man turn
When earth and sky neglect him?

Shall he reproach the late-coming rain,
Laggard, the lights are out and my servants departed?
Or say to the river, *Yesterday, had you run*
I had been here to receive you?
If a woman betrays him, there is relief in cursing,
But where shall he go or stay
When the rains are unfaithful?

II

The Drouth has taken the land!

On Mogollon the herd grass breaks in white tinder,
The Gila shows its bones, the Mimbres
Is a dried sinew on a shank too long uburied.

Over on Kaibab the blacktail
Browse on the bitter brush and the hemlock branches,
The round-horned elk have crossed over
By Wolf-creek pass to the lean ranges of Three Rivers.
Of the deer kind there is nothing left
Worth the chut of an arrow.

Around Tsotsil the buzzards
Are making a merry-go-round;
The rack-boned cattle
With their heads toward the stopped water courses

Are ringed with menacing shadows,
Nothing fattens now but the carrion eaters.

The disks of the prickly pear
Thin and curl like old pasteboard.
Down all the dark *bajadas* the hot wind has raped
The thousand-belled *maguey*,
And the White Ladies, the Dasylirion,
Who used to bow there and courtesy,
Scattering scent from their laces.
There's never a leaf-bird hops in the straked corn,
Never a flick in the one leaved pines, of the *piñonero*,
Nor a magpie, bringing the junipers,
Black and white on its wings, the footsteps of morning.
And dr-r-ry, dr-r-ry, dr-r-ry churrs the night hawk.

In the Rio Grande country
The starved mesas tug at the sky
Like calves at the stripped dugs of their mothers;
All day the saffron-colored winds struggle woundedly
For a few drops, scant and unrelieving
As tears to the aged.

Truly, Drouth has taken the land!

III

Oh, to see the fine rain walking
Among the Tewa villages
In her lilac-tinted veils!

Or the he-rain, upright between the ranges,
With his moccasins of dark cloud,
With his wings made out of the far darkness,

With his wing hollows out of the evening blueness,
With his voice of the thunder, *Thona*! *Thona*!
The voice of the rain standing.

O fructifying male divinity,
With the full-shaped cloud under thy feet,
With thy far-flung lightnings,
Come to us, soaring!

In Papagueria the mocking-bird
Is climbing his slender ladder of song
To the rain home, to the house of the dark cloud;
Down its viewless steeps his song comes dropping
Clear notes of roundness for the rain to follow.

In the west the clouds come up,
The white house of the rain comes up,
Thundering and shining,
Trailing ropes of rainbow the rain comes rushing!
Over the vast *abras* that are like charmless women
Aching to be coupled with the covering storm,
The rain comes roaring,
On the moon-colored *playas* the uneasy dust
Is laid by the holy rain.
Around the roots of the juniper
It makes slithery yellow runnels,
It gurgles in the *acequia*,
The great corn plant rejoices.

When shall we see this again!

IV

High on Jemez there's a great world shrine;
Looking north toward Pímpije,

Looking west toward Tsíkumu,
Looking south toward Óku and the Tewa world.
Deep bite the trails of the many, many moccasins
Working toward the shrine,
The white shell shrine of the six world regions,
And the four earth altars.

In the Tewa villages they are tying prayer plumes
For the shrines of Jemez.
They are burning candles to Moorish-eyed Madonnas
Pranked in Spanish hoopskirts,
To the carved and painted Santos,—
José with his flowering rod,
Jesus crowned with cactus,—
Little wavering candles.
They are making meal roads,
Ancient, holy roads for their prayers to pass.

In the Queres villages
The knowing ones are dancing,
Cloud-calling head-dresses blossom to the breeze;
Around the planted fields all the gourds are rattling,
Roll of prisoned pebbles like the myriad feet of rain!
They are dancing to the gods of the many-colored zenith,
To the old, kind gods of the gracious hidden faces,—
Hidden in the cloud masks, hidden in the rainbow—
Going to and fro to make the earth more fruitful,
To the dark cloud people,
To the arrow lightning people,
They are calling to the thunder
To bring the growing rain.

They are calling on the Host
By the drumhead's mimic thunder,
On the placid patron Saint in his pink crepe kimono,

With the silver clash of shells
Like the rapid rush of rain,
On the Blessed Ones and martyrs
Who come flocking to the drums,
On the new strong gods who make the Roman sign.
They are calling with their dancing,
Rain! Rain! Rain!

V

The Drouth is over the land.

This year six hundred Papagos
Who were once good cattle owners
Will be working the mines at Ajo.

On Moencopie a thousand flocks, unshepherded,
Will hear, for the voice of the herder,
The hunting cry of Mokiach, my lord Puma.
Dry farmers in Estancia,
Leaving their locked homesteads,
Are doubly shamed as they go, by the imploring
Stark arms of their orchards.
There is no weather sign watched now
By the citizens of small towns
But the tightening lines around the lips of their bankers.

We are in the Left Hand of God.

Thus said Our Ancients,
When of his inknowing thought Awillowillona
Made the earth mother, made the sky father,
Set them to spin in the midst of the world-encompassing water.
As in the Kiva the cloud-priest
Lifts with his breath the spume of the cloud-bowl,

So with his beam the Father-All-Father
Impregnates the foam cap.
Thus between sea and sun are begotten
The Great Twin Brethren, Righthand and Lefthand,
Up through the corn, pulling the dust to be man,
Pulling man down to the dust.

By what drouth of the spirit
Do we wallow so long in the dust,
Awillowillona!

Editor's Notes

Southwest Review 11 (January 1926): 116–20.

Several terms appear in the glossary of *Land of Journeys' Ending* (1924): *abra*, wide-open valley; *acequia*, irrigating ditch; *bajada*, down throw of a hill, steep slope; *maguey*, the century plant; *Moencopie*, place of running water, Arizona; *playa*, beach, land smoothed by water; *piñonero*, jay bird. For mythological background, especially concerning the twins appointed to be humankind's helpers, see the chapter "The Left Hand of God" in *Land of Journeys' Ending.* Most of the place names evoke pueblos and their cultures in New Mexico and Arizona. *Tsotsil* is the Navajo name for Mount Taylor, west of Santa Fe, New Mexico.

Not to You Only, O Pythian

Not to you only, O Pythian,
Out of rock crevices,
Out of earth's sacred middle
Where the ancient spore of the Sun
Still works in her,
Comes madness.

Here, out of Arroyos Hondos,
Between the prevailing
Stiff stems of the junipers,
Dream shaping vapors set back the moonlight,
Here from the wine red rift of the rim-rock,
Weighting the eyelids,
Out of the Grand Canyon's motionless unreality,
Visions prophetic.

Not to you only, the wish-colored
Word Hieratic,
Not solely at Delos, O Pythian,
But here at the desert's fire new edges,
Inebriate of the earth, to the Sun corybantic,
The god with my voice declaring
What I discern not.

Editor's Notes

Nation, December 8, 1926, 601.

Pythian refers to the oracle at Delphi and to the temple of Apollo there. Delos is the island traditionally thought of as the birthplace of Apollo and Artemis. Arroyos Hondos refers to the Arroyo Hondo Pueblo, at over a thousand inhabitants one of the single largest pueblos in the fourteenth century, located just southeast of Santa Fe, New

Mexico. The term may also suggest a landscape of "deep gullies" as inspiring as that of ancient Greece.

Puye

I

Here, say our father's fathers,
Out of the Womb-world, out of Sipapu, climbing
By the roots of the royal pine,
Came the First people.

Mother naked, sandal shod,
Hollowing their homes in the cliff side,
Fencing them with junipers.
In those days they were instructed of the juniper,
Whose boughs springing back taught them the bow play
While the reeds by the waterholes sang to them of arrows,
For whose feathering they gathered
Eagle plumes on Puye.

In those days the rains were plentiful,
The deer also, with their spotted fawns
Feeding on yellow flowers;
And the tall bucks cropping the young growth
At the ends of the blue spruce branches.
Here then, as now, was silence,
And the wide outlook whence the rains came,
With their wing feathers edged with dark cloud,
With the far-flung lightnings over their heads
And green, flowery footprints.
Where are they now, those Ancients?

Where are the wapiti, the round horned elk
They watched moving in the deep arroyos,
Like a bare wood, walking?

II

After these came the Small-House People,
Say the old men.
Very wise this People, People of the Seed,
Having received it from the Six Corn Maidens.
They laid up walls four-square, roofing them with aspens,
Kivas they built, underground, remembering the Womb-
world,
Dark Sipapu and the Black Lake of Tears.

Not ours, but kin to us, the Small-House People,
Giving honor to Awányu, the great plumed serpent,
Guardian of the water springs, to whom the rains are
friendly.
For them corn sprouted in the open spaces,
The fragrant bean plant and the gaudy squashes.
Wise were they of guile; came the deer to their singing,
While their women made them pots of painted borders,
And bore many children.

III

Here came our fathers,
Say the song priests,
Came the Tewas, came the Queres,
Moving south and ever south, so the clans may prosper,
Say the old men.

Not as the Small-House People came our fathers,
Every man to his own roof and the field between them,
But as a mother-hive, bound by the hearth keeper;
Wall touching wall and all the smokes commingling.
Still at Tyuoñi, cut above the door holes

Are the clan signs of the Queres,
But our fathers built at Puye.

Happy were our fathers, greatly did they prosper,
Dancing to the *tombes* and the deer hoof rattles
Till they brought the rains over Jemez,
The he-rain and the she-rain on Chirígi;
Till they heard the runnels gurgling
Round the roots of the great corn plant
And the lovely melon flowers.

Friendly, very friendly were the Small-House People;
Learning Tewa wisdom, they drew their homes together;
Round the rock of Puye ranged the Tewa hearth holes;
So the towns were builded.
Very many towns, and we talked across the housetops
By the smoke signs and the *tombes*
Návawi and Shufiné, Óttowi and Tsánkawi,
Calling them to Puye.

Noble was our Pueblo, north house and south house,
Far across Chirígi stretched our *temporales*,
Round the tasseled corn blue butterflies were dancing
As our fathers danced for rain and gave praises to
        Awányu.
Long was that time, very long,
Say the old ones,
Hip deep the trails between Óttowi and Tsánkawi,
Deep the trails on Puye.

Where are they now, those light stepping moccasins
Bit the rock walled trails between the happy Pueblos?
Where are the pronghorns that like shadow clouds
        in summer
Skimmed across Chirígi?

*

Faithless were our fathers,
Say the snake priests,
Pride was in their hearts and their thoughts left
            the straight road,
Pride of field and housetop, terraced ever skyward;
And no praises for Awányu.
Left they the dance and the secret Kiva vigils,
Sang they of love, and of war and wounding,
Black were their prayer sticks, raven plume and owl feather,
Black prayers for Puye.

In those days Awányu,
Say the old, old men,
Left the Tewa land where no longer sacred meal roads
Traced the spirit path to the four world quarters,
And men's hearts had left the straight road;
Left off honoring Awányu.
High across the heavens in disdain he flung him,
In the middle heaven white his ghost goes writhing
All across the midnight
Over Puye.

Then the rains walked not, and the water springs failed
And the hot winds danced on Chirígi.
. . . See that mound that the herdgrass scarcely covers
And the lean cactus cannot bloom upon?
That was once the Town of Yellow Flowers . . .
Even so with Puye.

Deeply lessoned, then our fathers
Built their towns anew by the rivers, built acequias
For the watering of the corn and the squashes;
Vainly beat the *tombes*,
Calling on the rain by the magic of their singing,

Calling on Awányu, who from heaven where he flung him
Seldom hears them.
Shrunken are our fields, shrunk the Tewa people,
And our hearts are withered.
While again the lizard darts
And the raven blackly stalks
And the Whiteman comes to stare
On Puye.

Editor's Notes

Nation, February 23, 1927, 202–03.

Many place names and allusions refer to specific pueblos, to Pueblo religion, to archeology and history of the Pueblo cultures in northern New Mexico, and to Austin's own account of Pueblo cultures in *Land of Journeys' Ending*. From the glossary of *Land of Journeys' Ending*: *Tombes* are ceremonial drums. *Puye* is the ancient cliff city near Espanola, New Mexico. *Awányu* is the plumed serpent deity. *Kiva* is the ceremonial chamber of the Pueblos. *Temporales* are rainstorms. *Sipapu* is the underworld of the Pueblos and the place of emergence, symbolically represented by the kiva.

I Have Known Poets

I have known poets in my time. . . .

I have also known a Cardinal,
A gold-laced General,
A Cabinet Minister and several millionaires,
Learned men, lover men—
And I would lose the lot of them
For any one of half a dozen poets that I know!
And I say, Lord,
When my time comes to go,
I shall not care for Heaven if the poets stay outside.
You may keep my starry crown
For some poor soul that craves it,
And give my harp
To any Angel child that plays it,
But I will take the poets and what you have left over,
A windy hill to walk upon, a filmy cactus flower,
A maple tree, a lady fern or bee caroused in clover,
Of all I've loved and sung about just the odds and ends—
And two or three poets to be my friends!

Editor's Notes

Nation, February 8, 1928, 156; reprinted in *Literary Digest*, March 10, 1928, 38; in Sioux City, *Iowa Journal*, April 22, 1928; and in *The Best Poems of 1928*, selected by Thomas Moult (London: Jonathan Cape, Ltd. 1928), 69.

Resurrection

Now, I said, that I am done
Even with sorrow—
Never any more yesterday nor to-day,
Never to-morrow;
Now that the worm, resentment,
Hath eaten my heart out wholly,
I will stretch out in its empty husk,
I solely,
Uncompanioned by grief or hope or wonder,
Knowing life only as the word
Death pronounces,
Crushing its dry husk under.

Here in my eyeless void,
Emptied even of my pulse's stirring,
Darkling I heard
Earth's timeless axles whirring,
From seas unreckoned
The foam-slavered sea pack
Yelp on the moon's cold traces;
Low in their places,
I that was done with wonder
Heard the unhurrying grasses
Lisping their leaves asunder.

Editor's Notes

Atlantic Monthly, April 1928, 529; *Literary Digest*, April 14, 1928, 32.

Pressure

In the middle street of my city,
In the broad street, men walk uprightly,
Their shoulders are thrown back,
Their bodies bulge smoothly frontward
Making room for the little god
That lives in all men's middles
To show the way to the broad streets
And the cleared spaces.

But in my street,
Where my home is and my children play,
Where the blades sprung from dropped dung
And the house sparrows contending
For grains between the feet of the dray horses,
Make a wild park for pleasure,
In that street all men go stooping,
As if a heavy hand pressed
Forever between their shoulders.
I, too, am bent over.

I remember I was young once
And thought I should always walk the broad streets
With my shoulders back.
But now the little god in me, pinched with my stooping,
Has forgotten his way about.
Think not that I have succumbed to any weakness;
I have gone down before the pressure,
Never to be out run or cast off,
The pressure of a heavy hand between my shoulders,
The Hand of Want.

Editor's Notes

Nation, June 6, 1928, 645.

Sounds

There is a sound of going
  in the tops of the mulberry trees,
The sound of a last breath.
In the cottonwoods also
And the willow-leafed poplars,
That a week ago were flame-pointed,
A sound as of bent blades clashing rustily.

There is a sound of going in the chamise
The sound of a besom sweeping, sweeping,
A sound of unconsidered things
Scurrying to brief corners of oblivion.

But with the spruce trees it is not so,
Nor with the balsam firs by the water borders.
A staying sound,
As of roots that strain but loose not
From the rock crevices.

I will go up to the evergreen pines,
To the blue spruces around Eagle Rock
And hearten myself with the sound of the star-built firs.

Editor's Notes

Chamise is greasewood (*Adenostoma fasciculatum*).

First of four "Southwestern Poems" in *Poetry*, June 1928, 123–27.

Caller of Buffalo

Whenever the summer-singed plains,
Past my car window,
Heave and fall like the flanks of trail-weary cattle,
When the round-backed hills go shouldering down
To drink of the western rivers,
And dust, like ceremonial smoke,
Goes up from the long-dried wallows,
Then I remember the Caller of Buffalo.

Then I think I see him,
Head-feathers slant in the wind,
Shaking his medicine robe
From the buttes of Republican River,
At Pawnee Bluffs
Offering sacred smoke to the Great White Buffalo.
Then at dawn, between jiggling curtains, I wake
To the star-keen note of his deer-shin whistle.

O Caller of Buffalo!
Hunt no more on the ancient traces
Pale and emptied of going as a cast snake-skin.
Come into my mind and hunt the herding thoughts,
The White Buffalo
Of the much desired places.
Come with your medicine-making,
O Caller of Buffalo!

Editor's Notes

Second of four "Southwestern Poems" in *Poetry*, June 1928, 123–27.

Caller of Buffalo

When past my car window
Summer singed plains are heaving
Like the flanks of trail weary cattle,
When the round backed hills go shouldering down
To drink of the western rivers,
And heat waves dance in the long dried wallows,
Then I remember the Caller of Buffalo.

Then I think I see him
Headfeathers slant in the wind,
Shaking his medicine robe
From the buttes of Republican River,
At Pawnee Bluffs
Offering sacred smoke
To the Great White Buffalo.
At dawn between the jiggling curtains
Comes the clear and star keen note
Of his deer shin whistle.

O Caller of Buffalo
Hunt no more on the ancient traces
Pale and emptied of going as a cast snake skin.
Come into my mind and hunt the herding thoughts,
The White Buffalo of the much desired places,
Come with your medicine making,
O Caller of Buffalo!

Editor's Notes

AU 55 typescript.

Rio Abajo

In Rio Abajo ghosts walk,
At Socorro I saw them,
Three and twenty brown gowns, rope-girt and sandalled.
By old Isleta ford,
Don Francisco de Coronado with his Spanish gentlemen—
Armor-rust on their satin sleeves,
Arrow-slits in their leathern greaves—
Rode all down the cotton fields
While the Tegua war-drums thundered.

Once in the dawn below Belen
Creaked the broad-wheeled carreta train
Whose single guttering candle showed
Where La Conquistadora rode
To reconquest and old pain.

Once by this saguan's ruined arch
Music its walls absorbed gave back again,
As in the dusk guitars were playing,
And on the stamped adobe floor
The dance still swaying.
Still is the Alameda sweet
With sun-steeped petals strewn
Where late the twinkling monstrance passed,
Mid gold more lucent than its own,
To bless the fields again.

Editor's Notes

Third of four "Southwestern Poems" in *Poetry*, June 1928, 123–27.

Rio Abajo is the lower Rio Grande River in New Mexico; Socorro is a New Mexican pueblo and town, named after Our Lady of Succor; *carreta* is a cart; *saguan*, usually spelled *zaguan*, is a passageway leading from the entrance door to the central patio in houses found commonly in the Southwest.

Litany for New Mexico

Bless God for the day!

Bless Him for the wide clear-flowing
New Mexico morning,
Poured round the shadow pools,
Gilt on the cumbres.

Bless Him for the nooning,
When the white thunderheads with sails full bowing
Sleep on the three wind rivers.
Bless God and praise Him
For the west-sloping hour of siesta
Under domed cottonwoods,
That in a rainless land make ever the sound of rain.

Bless Him for the evening;
For the releasing cool hands of the wind
On the flushed headlands;
For the lilac and larkspur veils
Let down by the mothering mountains
Between the work that fails and the dream that lingers.
Bless Him for home-coming sounds—
The window-shine on the loma,
For the welcoming flame and the savory smell
And the snuggling cry of the children.

Bless God for the night!

Bless Him for the keen curled sickle that reaps
The saffron meadows of the sun's late sowing;
For the full-shaped globe of wonder,
Pacing the eastern ranges.
Oh, bless Him more than all

For the ever recurrent orb that emerges
Between the light that goes and earth's oncoming shadow.

Bless Him for shared sleep,
For the midnight's healing fountain,
For the companionable cock-crow, warning
The sleeper back from dreams to the pastures of morning.

Bless God for the dawning,
For the earth collecting
Darkness again to her breast,
For the hills resounding
Clarion blue to the sun's relucence.

Bless God and praise Him
With exceeding thanksgiving
For His gift of the day and the night!

Editor's Notes

Fourth of four "Southwestern Poems" in *Poetry*, June 1928, 123–27.

AU 305 includes two reprints of the *Poetry* text: in *Literary Digest*, June 23, 1928, and in the *Providence (RI) Journal*, June 24, 1928.

Love Coming Late

Love came to me late,
having sent on before him
all his great company.

Young Love with his perfumed torch
beguiling the senses;
Passion, whose feet when I kissed them
blackened my mouth;
Duty which galled me worst
where the hurt was sorest.

Then with the sound of wings
down-edged for silence,
With a stir as of evening primroses blowing
wide apart among orchard grasses,
Secret, contained and aware,
Great Love came walking.

Came and sat down at the loom
where I stooped overwearied,
Swift were his hands and light on the shuttle;
And suddenly, as he wrought,
Duty and Passion and Youth
came back and served him!

Editor's Notes

Nation, July 11, 1928, 43.

Three at Carmel

I

How white the beach at Carmel was that day!
Woman white and curving round the discarded
    sapphire-shot, silk dappled heap of her garment
That lisped and lifted, bowed full to the wondrous long line
    of her, lapsed and revealed her.
Behind us the dunes breasted shoreward,
Moon cusped to the tussocks of tawny pale, trumpet shaped
    mimulus and apple-hued sea grass.
Low on the foreshore, Jack London and Sterling and I together.

Flickered the drift wood fire, copper, steel blue,
    and splints of emerald.
Voices of women darted and swerved like swallows or
    poised for our question and answer.
For one of us was a poet, and one
New come from the Sea Wolf's adventure,
And one had walked with the Trues in the land
    of Lost Borders.

If I told what the Trues had said, to Jack London
Who might just have come ashore there
From the Long Serpent, eyes blue as sea ice, bright
    as the sun blink on the Arctic ledges,
If Jack believed, or disbelieving, prophesied in the name
    of economic determinism,
Or if Sterling lifted the face Jack said was a Greek coin
    run over by a Roman chariot,
And demanded of Chaos an answer to man's unsearchable pain;
Who forgets, who remembers, when words are merely the
    twang of the string to the spirit's speeding?

Suddenly the bay, smit by the low sun's wheeling flanges,
Burst in green fire, with ash-flecked edges,
And Sterling unfolding his lean length leaped from his
 clothing like a young white scimitar cleaving the breakers,
Crying, The sea, the sea!
And the rest followed.

II

I remember the walk through the woods, the secret look
 of the pine boles,
Warm hollows between live oaks where amber lilies float
 in the wine of light,
The flower foam at the edge of Sterling's meadow;
The wind out of Sur with the smell of wild honey and
 yerba buena, answering each to each like speech;
Bursting spray heads over Lobos, torn surges revealing
 between gulfs in Time's outer garment, timeless
 sea gardens.
Oh, ever remembered, the incense smelling, resilient
 cypress boughs where we lay;
The perpetual flicker of talk, life litten, like the flick of
 the wind and the sun overhead in the pines' long needles.

Who that sat by them ever forgets the pitch pine fires?
And Jack London, ringed with admirers
Proclaiming the Social Revolution?
Or Sterling, alert and alien as a faun who has followed
 a slim-footed maiden home to her village,—
Whom the gods, for his disallegiance, have bound to the pure,
 austere service of Beauty,—
Between deep quaffs of social indignation, reading lines from
 the Wine of Wizardry and the House of Orchids!

III

How was the time unfaithful that they have left us?
Sterling self slain, not looking backward.
And Jack, for whom the Revolution to which his soul
        was a candle, proved laggard,
Guttering sootily out in his votive lantern.
Few there are who remember how we three raised the roof
        of Sterling's cabin
Till it burgeoned and grew to the Elder Ash Tree
While all the winged hopes of the world preened themselves
        in its branches.

Would they come back if they could to the spacious,
        work-filled mornings?
To the meals eaten in friendship,
Wine, which some undeserving quirk of my nature
        forbade me, and love play?
And for those two the releasing high moments of madness.
For Sterling, who followed the faun's way,
Had all the wild-creature instinct for his own besting.
Knowing his work done, and only Beauty immortal
He gave himself clean to Beauty;
Leaped from his garment of flesh as that day on the beaches
        naked he went to the sea.
So Beauty received him.

There I shall find him again, where Beauty awaits me.
If ever I walk in Carmel woods, if ever on Lobos,
I shall hear him shout in the morning surf undulant,
        sapphire sparkled.
I shall see him run with the warm noon wind where the
        leopard bright herdgrass wavers,
When the winds of Sur go wing and wing to evening blueness,
My friend shall come out as a star and I shall know him.

Saturday Review of Literature, September 29, 1928, 165.

Austin moved to Carmel in 1904 and helped establish a writers' colony there with Jack London (1876–1916) and George Sterling (1869–1926), among many others. Sterling was an acclaimed poet whose two most well-known books are *The Wine of Wizardry* and *The House of Orchids*. He was also the popular "King of Bohemia," but he ended his own life with cyanide at the Bohemian Club in San Francisco. At the age of forty, London died of kidney failure, aggravated by accidental morphine overdose. For good narratives of Carmel, see Stineman's biography of Austin, 84–105, and the more recent biography by Goodman and Dawson, 69–92.

Rio Abajo

In October the Valle del Rio Grande
Is a spate of copper, molten
Under bright scums of aspen-gold,
Green gold the frost refines
Till the beholder checks midway his gasp
Lest the force of an indrawn breath loose round him
The flood of exquisite disaster.

At Algodones the orchards
Shoulder like cows at the milking pen,
Patient but fain of the hand that strips them.
At Los Lunas
The vineyards are prone to the cruising flocks,
At Isleta the Rio
Thins finely to a gleam
Of harness metal on a roan stallion's flanks,
And all the glimmering ghosts
Of summer's bright impetalled hosts
Drift on the moveless air between its banks.

Editor's Notes

Saturday Review of Literature, April 12, 1930, 913.
Algodones, Los Lunas, and Isleta are three small towns along Interstate 25 near Albuquerque, New Mexico. The pueblos of Isleta, Santa Ana, and San Felipe are nearby.

The Dark Hours

I

In San Antonio de Quemado in New Mexico,
When the sound of snow water
Is heard in a hundred valleys,
When on the cumbres
Eaglets with mate-hungry eyes
Sit searching the larkspur-colored horizons,
In San Antonio de Quemado
They keep the Dark Hours in remembrance.

II

San Antonio was a pueblo once,
A walled and terraced pueblo,
But the Querechos sacked and burnt it.

Then came the Spanish men riding long-tailed elk
To the clank of iron clothing.
Then came the Brown-gowns bearing saving images,
Carved and lacquered vultos—
San Antonio for Quemado—
Whom for the sake of the Spanish guns against the Querechos
The Quemadeños kissed and accepted.
Still to be seen there in the mud-walled
Church of his dedication,
Between Our Lady of Innocence
And San Miguel of the Broken Toes—
So hard he stamped upon the devil
In Quemado.

Who knows when the name of the town was lost;
Or the Tano blood in the blood of Lopez, Vigil, Garcia;

Or why Maximilian died against a wall;
Or the Americanos came
And shut up the Querechos in reservations.

Only the years remained, and the vultos,
Somewhat chipped as to lacquer,
Serene by the unserved altars
Through the Dark Hours of New Mexico.

III

Surely the Saints—Isidro the Ploughman,
Santiago riding hard for God and New Mexico,
And that Moon-footing Lady
Who from the rocks of Tepeyac
Brought roses to bloom for Juan Diego,
Worked on Los Hermanos Penitentes,
Till out of their dark hours broke,
As the white fire breaks from the wild plum thickets
Along the creek borders,
Man's ancient incurable passion of expiation.

From the first Wednesday in Lent to Good Friday,
Among the little towns of the Sangre de Cristo—
Questa, Talpa, Ranchos de Taos,
Cundio, Chimayo, Rio Media
(But I chose San Antonio de Quemado)—
When on the Loma the Lenten twilights
Are brittle and gleaming,
Icy rims on the pool of darkness,
From Prado, Placito and Llano
Two and two go the brothers
To the windowless low morada;
Pablo the goat-herd and Pedro the woodman,
Julio home from the mines, Felipe and Juan from the ranchos,

*

There is no one now
Who is not worth something
Since now Christ has died,

Sing Los Hermanos Penitentes,

Come in on your knees and endure
The blood of his discipline.

Two and two go the brothers on the Rastre de Sangre,
To the slither of crosses dragged in the dust
And the steady fall of the flagels,
While the Compañeros sing, and Vicente,
Whose side is sealed with the bloodier patriot rites,
Carries the lantern.

He was the best man
That ever was on earth,
Let us now heartily endure
The stripes of His discipline!

Sing the Penitentes.

IV

What way shall the humble walk
In the cloud of their own unknowing
But the way of the Ancient Good,
Not understood but felt
In the stripes of mimic anguish.

Aside in the orchards
The sap of the pruned bough drips,
The ewes in the lambing pens

Shudder the way of life giving life,
And the women awake in their beds,
Hearing the flutes go by;
Eerie with nameless guilt
Persuasive of grief's assuagement,
Cross themselves and remember
How nothing comes to birth but by pain and endurance.
And pray to San Antonio de Quemado
For the spirit's safe deliverance.

Editor's Notes

Poetry, November 1930.

The glossary to *Land of Journeys' Ending* defines *cumbre* as *crest*. Two chapters in *Land of Journeys' Ending*, "The Saints in New Mexico" and "The Trail of the Blood," give good background for the poem and the "rastre de sangre." A *morada* is a lodge, the chapter-house of the penitents. The indigenous Mexican Juan Diego had a vision of Our Lady of Guadalupe at Tepeyac.

Cold Spell

Flat lands of Kansas,
    undulant, snow sleeked hollows
    endlessly bared to the cold's enchantment.

The sky is covered with feathers
    as of broody wood-pigeons.
Down, sifting over the plate round pools
    and candid, low-marged rivers,
Weights down the sedges;
    where now no mallard cries,
    nor teal nor widgeon.
The steers in the feeding yards
    mill with insistent
    maimed instincts of flight;
In the wood lot, the rabbit
    lopes forlornly.

The days are under a spell;
    the mornings blink with red lidded eyes,
    and the evenings
    fall like dead birds
    from a wounded wood-pigeon sky;
At midnight, the snuffling wind pack
    of the wide-seeking Witch Cold
    hunts and devours them.
At mid-day only
    the lit hearths of the homesteads
    hold mindlessly out against the cold's enchantment.

Editor's Notes

Harp, January–February 1931, 1.

The Aged Poet Discourses

Here by this round-head barrow,
Watching the shadow creep to the rose campion yonder,
I feel the pull of the time-stream. . . .

Long since it sucked from me all my male potency,
Creasing my shrunken belly with wave marks.

Here, in the sun-sleeked silence
My mind is loosed and aloft as an eyas,
Descrying my life in the time-stream,
Flaccid as weed, taking color and motion
From the sea's swindling mystery.

What becomes of that life, pulled free of its reef of being?

Not this body of my members,
But the body of wish and unwish, contacts, repulsions.
. . . There's nothing shores you in like a good hate,
As the scar of a wound holds when the clean flesh sunders.—
Here's all this for which my body is merely the—
The "plant." Exactly.
How you Americans do get a grip on the terms of materiality!
When the plant is duly resolved to salts and gasses
What becomes of the product, adrift in the time-stream
For any lackey of letters to piece into his livery?

Look what the penny curious have done to Shelley!

What was it I read yesterday of Heliodorus,
How he loved roasted turnips,
Or one of his mistresses had a skewed eyebrow?
That sort of thing! intact in the time-stream,
The Continuum, the Something, the Remembers—

Call it God then.
Could God remember the eyebrow of Heliodorus' mistress
And utterly loose Heliodorus out of his consciousness?
Say He forgot the way of a bird's wing in the air
Or my life's smallest instant?
Wouldn't the Universe come crashing together?
Suppose when I go under, some small wares
Loose in my mind's pocket, songs not quite shaped,
The temper I was in about my pudding yesterday,
Do come ashore, to be picked up by a professional ghost raiser,
At a dollar a ghost . . . ?

Totheridge, at the home farm there, lost a son at Ypres.
Corporal with scout detachment. Last thing they heard
Was his high, country sing-song,—
Come on you swine, you! Come— Then the shell burst.
Nothing, not even an eyebrow, recognizable.

Later one of these London mediums gets hold of the boy's mother.

As I understand it the medium runs up his own mind
Like a—what's the term? Aerial? Thank you—
Mixed with a lot of unintelligible patter,
Comes through the boy's name for his first dog,
And a trick his mother used to get him up mornings,
Thick with good country sleep.
But is that the sort of thing
A discarnate intelligence concerns itself about?

Touching Totheridge's case, I admit
After such a storm as this war, there'd be wreckage.
Hours on my quiet lawn, when Totheridge's cows
Form single file at the gatehead, and round-voiced maids
Come thudding their pails in the dew,
Thoughts of our simple, south country lads

Troop homeward, like doves to their proper cotes.
You've noticed? There's a sadness since
Falling through all the pleasant air of England.

. . . This new concept of Time as the measure of Consciousness
Tracking its way through space . . .
Lying awake at night
Through great arcs of the earth-swing,—
So well have I learned my task of awareness
I need very little sleep to rest me from it—
Death seems merely the notice of disembarcation,
From which we find ourselves
High on the coast of eternal Nowness.

Wouldn't millions of us, if we could,
Scurry back into the time-stream
Like sand hoppers from a high flung wave mark?
Wouldn't we go haunting the spot of our disembarcation,
Familiarly spaced with a past, present, and future?

Yesterday Hernshaw and I
Talked as men talk after forty years of friendship,
As moored boats in a fairway
Jib and fall with a self-same motion,
Talked and were still. All at once, and surely,
I was aware of a Presence, hailing me softly
By an old name and precious.

Hernshaw's rose-slip daughter . . . budded out of his flesh . . .

Twenty years since she left us,
Taking love too hard and life too lightly.
Suddenly, there she stirred, where I was closest,
Inside him. . . .
As a flower unclosing in darkness

Touches the sense by nuances too slight for naming.
"Alice!" I answered.
Hernshaw soothed me, "Alice is dead, you know."
Thinking I maundered.

What's dead, but set free from Time-space?

Where else could she go, by timelessness affrighted
Whom her own time so dismayed?
I remember her first excursions from my chair to his,
Not essaying the path till Hernshaw's hand
Made it warm and familiar . . .
Back from the Now she had slipped to the safe shape of his being.

Shall we be free, indeed, who are not affrighted,
Ranging the centuries as children a brookside?
Or seek by some such compulsion
As drives the sea trout to the waters that spawned him,
Through infinite, curved spaces,
Till we have absorbed all times into ourselves
And so achieved Godhead?

Editor's Notes

Saturday Review of Literature, August 29, 1931, 86.

An *eyas* is a young hawk taken from the nest for the purpose of training.

maunder = to think or speak incoherently.

Home Thoughts in the City

Was it a steam ratchet that I heard,
Or did my parrot shriek?
Stale gust of gullied street,
Or mesa wind that stirred
The sharp-edged yucca shadows
That like drowned weed along the smooth adobe wall
Swim in the heat's high tide of moving jade,
While like a crab the green and scarlet bird
Sidles from deep to deep of tawny shade?

When the mind wills, how thin a blade of sound
Lets through the fragile lisp of bougainvillea leaves,
Or ripe fruit dropping on the grassless ground!
How brief an instant turns
The traffic's slithering stream
To the acequia madre's slow ensilvered gleam!

Outside the Zaguan's arch the foothill trail
Winds up to seek
Bluc altar-lifted mesa and remote cowled peak,
Through spined and brittle chaparral, where frail,
Bright trumpets of the mimulus
Answer contented pipings of sleek quail.
And where the woodman with his burro pack
Trudges between chamisa and choyital,
Rises a pagan wind and casts
The dust of imprecation on his track.

Editor's Notes

Folk-Say IV: The Land is Ours, ed. B. A. Botkin (Norman: University of Oklahoma Press, 1932), 91.

Mountain Parable

A mountain is a parable
Told in the twilight by Earth Horizon
To the little, low huts on the loma;
Huddled huts like little children
As they watch their mother going
In her robes of evening splendor
And her shining yellow shoes,
Going to the Sun's house,
Very loth to let her go, but rejoicing in her beauty.
Little huts along the loma
With their hands about their knees and their heads upon them,
While the ancient Earth Horizon
Speaks to them a parable.

Once in a world way, says the Earth Horizon,
All the sacred mountains
Issued from the Cloud Bowl,
Young they were and virgin,
New come to life, the dance of life was on them.
Dancing with the foam cloud,
Dancing with the rain cloud,
The mountains bared their breasts
To the Sun's enchantment;
Young strong Sun,leaping on the mountains.

Thus runs the parable:
Heavy grew the mountains with the sun fruit;
Left they their dancing;
Trees they bore and villages;
Furrowed grew their breasts feeding broods of hills,
Feeding pleasant corn lands;
Grave grew the mountains, grave and self-encompassed.

Lean against the mountains, all you little villages!
Says the Earth Horizon.

Drowsy are the huts on the loma
Looking toward the west
Where the many-colored blanket of the Day streaks and darkles,
And they see between their eye-winks how the mountains
Are dancing on the cloud rim,
Dancing to the Sun's house to renew their maiden promise.
Trusting in the mountains,
With their heads upon their knees
Sleep the little huts on the loma.

Editor's Notes

Folk-Say IV: The Land is Ours, ed. B. A. Botkin (Norman: University of Oklahoma Press, 1932), 91–92.

A *loma* is a broad-topped hill or ridge (*Oxford English Dictionary*).

UNPUBLISHED POEMS AND FRAGMENTS

The fifty-three texts collected here can be found in the Mary Austin Papers, housed in the Huntington Library in San Marino, California. They are arranged by the Huntington's folder numbers, in a roughly alphabetical order. The Austin Papers (AU) are divided into dozens of archival boxes, in which the researcher finds dozens of numbered folders. There are doubtless other manuscript and typescript poems to be found in other repositories, but this section gives a good representation of the poems Austin wrote throughout her career. Some date from her earliest years, and she claimed that they were written when she was no more than ten years old. Others date from the very end of her life. Many can be dated as coming from the Santa Fe years because they are typed on sheets bearing the name of Austin's home there, Casa Querida, or the names of Mary Austin and Santa Fe themselves.

The number of carbon copies suggests that Austin maintained a serious interest in writing poems until her death. She kept the carbon copies in order to make corrections and have her secretary retype the texts for her. Some folders show poems in a number of stages of composition; others contain a single fair copy or a single carbon copy. In a very few cases, such as the late poem "By the Deer's Cry," I have taken the liberty of reconstructing a reading text from drafting fragments or worksheets. In other cases, I have made silent editorial choices concerning which of several drafts to use as a copy text. In no case, however, have I changed Austin's language.

The unpublished work reveals, once again, a writer with a wide range of interests, both formal and thematic. The Southwest and Native American culture remain prominent, but there are also a number of poems about the seashore, about current social events, and about the dreams of a young woman writer in California. In short, the section suggests yet another version of Austin's long career as a practicing poet.

The Camp Fire

When the night comes walking, walking in the meadows
On the shut-eyed purple gentians by the creek,
When the tallest peaks cast taller, slimmer shadows,
And the long last-lighted slopes are grey and bleak;
When a lost wind whimpers, fumbling for the clearing,
And the water noises fall off half a tone;
When the star fires through the dusk the peaks are nearing,
Then 'tis time to light a camp fire of your own.

Then 'tis time to set the sapless logs a-roaring,
Stir up flames to whip the darkness till it flees,
While the merry, crackling sparks go star-ward soaring
Like the feathered folk that twinkle through the trees.
Then the shouting flame drops off for better hearing
When the cougar screams and whines beside his lair,
And the flesh along your back crawls up with fearing
And you heap up pitchy boughs to make a flare.

Then you curl up on your bed of springy needles,
Lie up snug to watch the heart-wood glow and char,
While the water in the runnels purrs and wheedles,
From the meadow where the folded lilies are.
Only wake to hear the wood folk, round you going,
Thread the pine boles with small noises low and least,
See the embers in the wavering ash heap glowing
Red and winking, like the eyeballs of a beast.

Editor's Notes

Typescript, corrected and retyped; *AU* 57, from before 1912; an early typescript has Independence, California, as her address.

Campo Santo at San Juan

Come where the mesa's lion-colored paws
Set back the lordly Rio to the west,
And I will show you sleep!

Set round are magic mountains, blue on blue,
That thin to wreathing veils and are exhaled
By the out-breathing spirit of the universe
In pulse of lilac light;
Between them high stretched mesas, tombe tight,
Whereon the gods
Drum sullen thunder these hot afternoons
Till the plumed clouds come up like eagles
Dun-feathered, edged with white,
With arrow lightnings sheath'd in their claws.

A bow-shot nearer to the mesa's edge,
Pale huts that drink the sun;
Long after dark their walls give back warm tones,
The wine of light.
Five centuries and more these walls
Have been drawn out of dust by women's hands—-
They too have drunk the sun, are dusky with it,
Their white teeth give secret flashes, and their eyes,
The very fibers of their blankets sparkle
Clear red and yellow like stained glass.

Sit here by the Cacique's house
And watch Lupita plastering a wall
With dust that was some mother's son,
Mixed with the rain that fell, how many times,
As women's tears.
This was their life;

A wind that rose and struggled with the dust
And stilled to dust again.

Such changes came as overtake
These same stark mesas in a season's range;
Mere bloom of use and custom
Our unregardful time has blown away.
Where once the prayer-plume and the cloud-compelling drum
Circled the pregnant fields,
The five fiscales bear the village Saint,
And still for rain the six Corn Maidens dance
Round Mary Virgin in the market place.

And then, their little dust makes room
For the crepe-petalled argemony,
A potshard and a penciled word
Amado. . . . . Loved . .
Full fed of life, what need
To set a beggar's bowl for scraps
To round the measure of identity?

If dust could feel, their dust had but come home
To herd grass and to painted cup,
To crisping frost and slender-footed rain,
The great lord Sun returning from the South
Clad in white beads and shell shield glittering.—
And they are one with all they looked upon.

Editor's Notes

AU 58; four typescripts, one clearly the last, with Austin's name and that of her home in Santa Fe, Casa Querida.

Campo Santo is a cemetery. San Juan is a pueblo near Santa Fe, New Mexico. *Tombe* is a ceremonial drum. *Argemony* or *argemone* is the plant prickly poppy.

Charm Strings

Carmel Beaches

Moon glistered, naked shouldered dunes
Run up, hill pointed in the land wind,
Run down, wave hollowed in the sea gusts.

Frail umbels of sand verbena, yellow and lilac,
Strive with yesterday's shapes of crest or hollow,
But the beach grass subdues equally
Moon whiteness and undulant contour
By its unimpeachable virtue of dullness.

Santa Barbara

Between sea smelling windrows of weed
The ripple runners, the skimmers of foam,
Shearlings, black curlews, sandpipers
Nest under land adventuring grasses
That have still the sea's habit of bowing and flowing.

San Diego

White lady faces of chamise
Bowing and lifting make decorous response
To the sea's prophecy
And about their knees,
Where yellow violets run goldenly,
The flick of rosaries.

San Isidro

Red hills, robin breasted
And the young tamarisk's feathering green.

No grief can come
But I shall still be glad remembering
How the young robins sang
At San Isidro on the Jemez river.

Editor's Notes

AU 64; two of these poems were published in *El Palacio*: "San Jacinto" and "Ensenada Todos Santos"; see Magazine and Periodical Publications.

San Isidro is now spelled San Ysidro, a small but ancient village on the Jemez River in Sandoval County, New Mexico.

Choyital

Still, very still now;
Make no motion,
Let yourself go weightless
With abstraction;
Let your thought swim
Upon sleeping fin, indistinguishable
From its shadow,
Let the shadow even
Lie inert, as the yucca moth,
Its mating ended.

Still, go very still, let no feather
Stir on the dove smooth breast of appetence.
Let desire loose not
The least crepe flexure folded
Over the cinctured gold of argemone,
Lest between the riffle of a wing tip
On the smooth water-gloss of somnolence,
And the flick between two silences, they take you,
The spirits of the Choyital.

Fear not the sahuaro.
Not the organ fluted,
In-breathing, out-breathing,
Sibylline shape with thickened, uplifted,
Arms declaring the full diapason
Of life ascendant.
Not Siva, the many-handed, not Isis,
Multitudinous, teeming breasted
Gestured more amply
Out of stone, time rotted,
And the infertile slough of mesquite and cat-claw.

Fear not the falcon haunted sahuaro,
In whose arms the red-tailed hawk has nested.

But go fearfully about the choyital.

Go not where the impuissant land
Under the spined, indehiscent,
Fruiting tips of the choya
Crouches in rut, unslaked
By the furtive, inappetent
Rape of the cactus.
Where even the whoring grass
Is avid of avoidance,
Go not except cautiously.

Go in April,
When the white-pigeon petals of argemone
Flock on their grey green stems
Down the waterless washes:
When the woodpecker
Clucks from the door of his house
In the tall sahuaro
To the blue throated lizards, darting
Harmlessly up and down its organ flutings,
When the great hawks
Sail mated, hawk to shadow.

Go not to the choyital
When the noon is empty of motion;
Vacant the pack-rat's sill,
And the farmer-ants
Shut up their crystal doors
'Gainst the noon's enchantment.
Go not, when the rut of the earth augments

In the hot honey scent of the crimped,
Gold foil bloom of palo verde,
When the lust of the grass to be man—
Force, defrauded of substance,
God-head, naked of man,—
Rises fierce with denial, spined with the torment
Of fecundity unwombed, unbreasted.
Oh, go not to the choyital
Lest it come leaping upon you!

Editor's Notes

AU 69 includes three early drafts, a later draft, and a corrected final draft, on letterhead that reads "Mary Austin, Santa Fe, New Mexico," with two carbon copies.

For several of these terms, see the chapter "Cactus Country" in *Land of Journeys' Ending. Choyital* is properly *chollital*, where the cholla cactus grows; *argemone* is the prickly poppy; *palo verde* is the "green tree" of the Southwest desert; *sahuaro* is Austin's common spelling for the giant saguaro cactus.

[Dear are the little towns of the Sangre de Cristo]

Dear are the little towns of the Sangre de Cristo,
Lovely and rememberable:
Proud Cundio, the eagle's nest,
Quemada like a broody partridge
Beside the quilted fields,
Dear and rememberable—
Dear the three peaks of Truchas marching
Into the trackless sky

But dearer is Rio Chiquita;
The begigna rivers,
The old house like a falcon over
The cienagas,

The cherry trees like young girls with white pitchers,
The moon a silver fountain.

Editor's Notes

AU 105

Sangre de Cristo, the Blood of Christ, is a mountain in New Mexico. The towns are in the Santa Fe area. *Begigna* is a Spanish proper name for a woman. *Cienaga* or *cienega* is a swamp or wet meadow (*Land of Journeys' Ending*).

The Field of Glory

Oh, father, what of the stinking mist
That shakes to the sound of screaming,
And the skirl of the black and bursting rain,
And the angry fire spits gleaming?
Oh, what is it writhes in the reddened fields
When the mists are split by the thunder,
And what of the shrieking line that reels
And tramples the writhing under?

The raven answered his children three,
Gleeful, and hoarse, and hoary,
Oh, that is the children of men, said he,
Reaping the Field of Glory.

And what of the vulture folk anigh,
And the kite's slant piñons folding,
And what is it bodes in the wolf's long cry,
And the eagle's all beholding?
And what of the drip of your feathers red,
And the reek of your talons gory?
Oh, I have been with my kind, he said,
Gleaning the Field of Glory.

Editor's Notes

AU 155 contains the first draft and a revision, signed.

Fossils of the Tertiary

We were blind, dumb things in a shallow sea,
Shoals and shoals, and a thick, slow tide
That carried us where we would not be;
That shifted and stunted us helplessly
Through waters that weltered and wandered wide.

The deep called unto the deep elate,
The earth to the rain, the moon to the sea;
The primal forces knew love and hate;
The chemic atoms had each its mate;
There were none so hapless and lone as we.

But God had pitied us from his sky,
The long tides sifted us heap on heap,
The good earth yawned and the sea went by;—
The sea-silt covered us deep to lie
In the core of a hill for an age long sleep.

Until men came groping to read God's word
In the book of the earth where his word is writ,
How its beams were laid and the deeps were stirred,
And we found our burial heap preferred
For lo, God had marked a page with it!

Editor's Notes

AU 180; single clean sheet, typescript.

Lady Bug

Lady bug, lady bug fly away home
The scale bug is down in the orchard alone
He is eating his way to the topmost limb
Lady bug; lady bug! go and eat him.

Editor's Notes

AU 182; manuscript in a ledger with three other poems.

Austin claimed this poem as the original source for most of the verses in *The Children Sing in the Far West*. See "Poetry in the Education of Children," *MASW*, 213.

Gilia

White, O white are the gilia flowers,
As silently one by one,
They open their hearts in the evening hours,
To the westward wheeling sun.

Sweet, O sweet are the gilia flowers,
And the silly night moth knows
By their musky scent in the darkling hours
He finds where the gilia grows.

Editor's Notes

AU 182 and 205; this version follows the *AU* 205 text.

Love Song

Come when the young moon's saffron light
Streams over the distant hills,
And there falls no sound on the summer night
But the murmur of happy rills
Or the drowsy whirr of the night moth's wings
Mid the blossoms you cannot see;
Come softly under my window
And I will unbar to thee.

Come by the path where the alders glow
Milk white like nuns at prayer
And the place of the primrose beds you know
By the fragrance that lingers there
Come by gate where the jasmine vine
Climbs to the cypress tree;
Come softly under my window
And I will unbar to thee.

Touch but a note of thy light guitar
One sweet note soft and clear
And tho' I be dreaming my heart will wake
And tell me my love is near
Tho' thy step be light on the velvet lawn
As the dreaming moonlight be
It would speak to me under my window
And bid me unbar to thee.

Editor's Notes

AU 182 contains an envelope with Austin's explanation: "The enclosed is a stray leaf out of an old blank book in which I recorded my earliest verse. The love song is a fragment of something I wrote when I was about ten years old. I called it 'a play to be sung' never having heard the word opera. The original was not technically so correct but the idea was the same. There was a definite picture in my mind of a dark, nearly black stone house with a tower and spring bulbs blooming in the garden. Somewhere in the house were dark people plotting. I recall distinctly that the 'play' came to me in several distinct parts which I did not know enough to call 'acts,' and it worried me because it was not continuous action. I have never been able to trace this to anything I might have read at the time. It occurred before my father's death which was in my 10th year."

Fragments of Unidentified Manuscripts

"A Memory in Spring"

She who, departing hence, left to the flowers of the plum-tree,
Blooming beside our eaves, the charm of her youth and beauty
And maiden pureness of heart, to quicken their flush and
fragrance—
Ah! where does she dwell to-day, our dear little vanished sister?

"In a Cemetery at Night"

This light of the moon that plays on the water I pour for the dead
Differs nothing at all from the moonlight of other years.

"After Long Absence"

The garden that once I loved, and even the hedge of the garden,
All is changed and strange; the moonlight only is faithful;
The moon alone remembers the charm of the time gone by!

Editor's Notes

AU 185

Good Medicine

How well I know what I mean to do
When the snows are shed on the hill,
And under the drifts the tamarack lifts
The singing needles are still.
When the snows are so deep that the speckled grouse
Can perch on the broadest boughs,
And safe in the lee of a strong backed pine
The chilly robins will house.

I shall go to the Paiute medicine man
In his wickiup close by the creek.
He shall make me a singing medicine,
And this be the gift I shall seek:
That he shall divide my self in two
In the time old skill of his kind,
So while the shape of me sits by the fire
Far travels the self of my mind.

Then I shall go up where the shining drifts
Drop back from the rearing peaks,
By the shining sag in the meadow of snow
To follow the trails of the creeks.
And deep in under the blue white sludge
To tickle the dozing trout,
Where the brown bear sucks at his paws asleep
To know what he dreams about.

When the firs are bent in a wind built tent
And the boughs of the buckthorn lean
In a snow thatched arch to the boulders brown,
And the robins flit between,
I shall softly slip like an errant flake
In the swirling swarm of the snow,

And round by the peaks where the wind flood seeks
I shall find the things I would know.

Editor's Notes

AU 215: single clean sheet, typescript.

The Heaven of Songs

Old songs should not be kept
Pressed for remembrance in dim libraries,
Nor yet like doves,
Grown sick with fondling,
Freed from hands half weary.
But while their wings are keen to take the wind,
Before some critic huntsman brings them down
And what was once so silvery and fleet
Is rumpled plumage and the bookworm's meat.

I'm sure there is a heaven for old songs!

I know the way they'd take,
Up from the lucent pool, the flower starred path
Where seraphs lead
The happy monks of Fra Angelico.
Like maidens, with lithe hips and blossomed breasts
In singing bands they'd pass
Through Perugino's hills;
And then along the mellowed slope
Where once Giorgione's Venus pressed the grass.

Above their name-flowers, violet shod,
In crocus colored sleeves they'd flit,
Where still the Lesbian words
Redden like apples on the highest boughs,
And Georgian lyrics sip
At every rose-song's dew delighted lip
Like dozy golden bees;
Hurt canzones of Verlaine,
Their passions fallen like rain,
Drift as young gossamer along the morning sod.

Editor's Notes

AU 219: two corrected copies and a third, very clean, as here. Submitted to *Forum* on November 20, 1927.

How the Earth was Made at Pit River

In this place
Say the fathers of our fathers,
There was nothingness and void.
In this place
Wearily went the Eagle,
Wearily Coyote
Saying where shall our station be?
Where shall we rest?

Purposing inwardly, Earthmaker Coyote
Scratched at the void;
By effort and inknowing thought
Made dust out of nothingness,
Dancing he firmed it.

Around earth horizon
Four times they circled, Coyote and Eagle,
Three times to the place of earth's beginning
Returning unwearied.
Three times they widened the earth by their dancing
The fourth time returning
Wearily staggering,
"It is enough," said Coyote.

Said the Eagle,
"Wide is the earth, O Pad-foot,
But where shall a claw foot
Find perch and holding?
Lo, there shall be mountains!"

Busily scratched they,
Valleys and hills and sky-propping ranges,
Thus, said they twain, worlds should be fashioned.

Fast as they labored,
Such was the might of their world making magic,
Where fell an eagle plume, sprouted a pine tree,
Pinfeathers grew into buckthorn and berry bush,
Shed hairs of Coyote thickened as grasses,
Bright from their sweat leaped springs and rivers,
Thus in this place
Earth became, say the fathers.

Editor's Notes

AU 225: two drafts, neither one very clean, one incomplete, with only one correction.

In Hospital

Now I know that life
Is much more important than I had imagined.

God is not omnipotent!
He has not been able to create life
Easy to let go or to come by,
He has not been able to make healing
Grow beautifully out of the stroke of injury,
Nor Life giving life except to the rhythm of anguish;
He is not omnipotent.
Even to those who have life thrust upon them
He has not been able to convey the meaning of his invention,
He has not certainly made it known if life is immortal.

What does it matter then, about the count of the stars
Or the shape of the Universe,
Or that a man might fly past Betelguese
At a hundred miles an hour for a million years?
Life is important, because it costs so much,
Wherein we are admitted to secret sharing
Of God's incompetence, His last, least perfected adventure.
What does it matter that time goes chuckling in the dark
At the joke of eternity? It may be the man-soul will laugh
Out besting his creator,
Subduing the pain of birth and the anguish of dissolution,
It may be that I shall discover
The uninvented trick of immortality.

Editor's Notes

AU 234; two drafts, with little correction.

Invocation to Sleep

Come Sleep, O Lady Sleep,
From earth horizon,
From the far darkness
Come to me swiftly!

Come cover me with the breast feathers of oblivion
As a mountain is covered with cloud,
Let me be streaked with sleep
As the mountain with fine rain,
Till all my thought goes from me
And I am washed clean of remembrance.

Come, O Comfortress,
Come with your seven dark roses,
Lay them upon my eyeballs, seared
With seeing what I would not,
Cover my ears, astonied
With life's refusals;
Bind them upon my thought's thorn pointed insistence;
And the darkest, lay upon my heart.

Let me know sleep as a weight,
As the uncoffined feel earth pressure
Firming the stir of dissolution.

O Lady Sleep,
Priestess-enchantress, having lapped me
In seven fold blackness,
Show me thy cloak's lining.

Show me patterns of great queens stayed
By untouchable ancient loyalties
As heroes on locked shields

Of sweating soldiery.

Show me great courtesans
Safe curtained by golden rain
That with its mellow clinking muffles
The wolf howl,
Under whose fall unstinted
Never gnaws the mouse, anxiety.

Show me dead kings in rock chambers
Ringed with choice and subtle possession,
Necessaries subdued to the king's touch
With gold chased on ivory;
Wall pictures wherewith slaves assuaged
Insatiable lack; morning wind on the wild rice,
Waterfowl hazy with speed,
Lotuses of light

Such as loved women's faces bloom into.

O Sleep, at thy poorest
Let in the day-hunted quarry
To lair under thy thick garment
And lose for a space the sound of pursuing!

O Lady Sleep
Priestess-enchantress
Come to me swiftly!

Editor's Notes

AU 260: first draft and three subsequent drafts or carbon copies, all legible.

[It needs not that the dead should walk]

It needs not that the dead should walk
Or that behind the veil of things
We hear through dull and alien sense
The deathless beating of their wings.

Shall we who felt their spirits pulse
Before they wore the guise of form,
Not feel them through the aching dark
Against our bosoms beat as warm?

Oh, Child shall we who loved so well
Before you took or shape or breath,
Love less the years you wait for me
Beyond the formlessness of death?

Editor's Notes

AU 264: manuscript dated May 10, 1915, on stationery of the National Arts Club, New York City.

A Lesson

The wind it blew on Brierly Hill
Till the firs did creak amain,
And the storm wrack hid the things it did
In long grey gusts of rain.

The snows did press, the frost did bite,
And the wind it wried them still,
And the sleet and the rain went into the grain
Of the firs on Brierly Hill.

And that is the reason the star-built firs
Went down to the wind-blown main,
To prove on the sea what they learned to be
In the snow and the sleet and the rain.

Editor's Notes

AU 296; clean typescript, with "Shasta?" as potential place substitution for "Brierly Hill" but only in the first stanza.

[Let Me Go Forth]

Let me go forth,
Before the memory pales
Of other times than this
Ere blindly down the path of joy
We blundered into pain
To know no surcease of our wounded hearts
But wounding each again.

Beloved let me go,
While still it is my bitter balm to know
I could not hurt you so
Had you but loved me less.

Let me go forth,
And haply by my going bring release
As in torn forests when the great winds cease
The boughs spring back again.

Ere we forget how dear our love has been
Beloved let me go.

Editor's Notes

AU 297; untitled typescript.

Love in New England

Mary Abigail leaned out of the best room window
Of the old Pillsbury house,
And the peonies down the front walk, as the wind turned them,
Were as faces crowding the aisle when the bride passes.
In the dark of the currant bushes
Fireflies hunted their loves with lanterns,
From under leaf coverts
Green things fiddled to theirs,
And hylae trilled from the ends of maple branches.
O God, O God! sighed Mary Abigail,
Who had never done anything unworthy of a Pillsbury.

Down Locust Street Mariano the Portuguese
Sang as he strolled,
Having the same need of singing as the katydids and the hylae,

O bird of my heart, sang Mariano,
Why so far art thou nesting?

At the gate of the old Pillsbury house,
Clean white, green shuttered, pillared for hospitality,
Mariano cursed, recalling
How a dream of home-centered self-realization,
Delicately announced by the scent of the mock orange
Meeting over the fan light the cinnamon roses,
Had guided his people
Out of the hot muddle of peasant thinking
To the unassailable properties of Locust Street,
And the one lit window
Out of which leaned the last of the Pillsburys.

"Why so far, O bird of my heart," sang Mariano,
And O God, O God! moaned Mary Abigail

Like any wild thing calling for its mate, unanswered.
And over the old Pillsbury house the moon
Rose single and white as an uneaten sacrament.

Editor's Notes

AU 324: typescript and two carbon copies.

Love in New Mexico

It should have been there by the river,
By the Red buttes,
By the bridge of Otowi,
Where the lion colored river fawns and gurgles;
Thin green the flames of sycamore unsheathing,
And the lifting, blossom cymes of the pear trees
A white wound at the heart.
It should have been there that you loved me.

Ah, heard you not the horns of color blowing
From the tall potreros,
Orange, scarlet, golden,
Or the brazen, bassoon-throated lowing
Of the earth, desirous for the plough.
If you were here by the river
It should be now!

It should be at the peach tree's rosy signal,
In the lost ecstasy of petaled orchards,
While in mid air the broody mountains
Stoop whitely on furled wings, as eaglets
Covering their mates in March, along the cumbers.
What then were youth or age between us,
Or wealth or pride, or any other creature;
What were comeliness of men, or woman's beauty
Who, lost in Beauty's self, need not the seeming?
It should have been there
In the Valle del Rio Grande!

Editor's Notes

AU 325: typescript and three carbon copies, with some corrections.

Otowi is a Tigua pueblo ruin; *potrero* is a colt pasture, or any naturally fenced pasture; *cumbers*, which Austin also spells *cumbres*, are crests of a hill or ridge.

The Love of the World (1894)

I hope in Heaven there are silver firs
Grown straightly up by winding water ways,
And bud and bloom for seasons and for days.
The wind that through the herdgrass pasture stirs
The frost that pricks the pine tree's swelling burrs,
The bind-weed and the sulphur flower,
The owl that brings the gilia's hour,
The blundering moth that to the primrose whirrs.
I trust I shall not miss the meadow grass
From fields elysian, nor the wind-rung bells
Of columbine among the asphodels.
Nor dipping willows where the waters pass,
I have no mind for harps and seraph's wings,
'Tis Heaven for me with all green growing things.

If I could after death, which meaneth sleep,
Rid of the cumbering of this fleshly frame,
Come up this path whereby the poppies flame,
By hanging meadow and fir planted steep
With these wild loves of mine a tryst to keep,—
If I could, looking with new lighted eyes,
Some happy secret of their bloom surprise
I would not think that death were cause to weep.
If I could learn the mystery and the power
Whereby one soil makes perfume sharp or sweet,
If I could know what star-moved forces meet
In the rhymed season's flow of leaf and flower
No other heaven I'd ask, no more of earth
Than but to sing their meaning and their worth.

How shall I tune my voice to angel choirs
Who cannot speak the crooning river calls,
Nor catch one anthem of the chanting falls

Whose hymns outreach the fretted forest spires,
The storms that quench the sunset lighted fires
Along wild headlands when the summers wane,
And the long thunder, and the drumming rain—
More than my soul can compass, each inspires.
How reach the throne who cannot with all care
Proclaim the white evangel of the snow;
Though the soul struggles strongly panting so
All its great weight of wonder to outbear.
No dread apocalypse my soul can bow
To more of awe than bids it silence now.

Editor's Notes

AU 329

The Love of the World (1906)

I hope in Heaven there are silver firs
Grown straightly up by winding water ways,
And bud and bloom for seasons and for days.
The wind that through the herdgrass pasture stirs
The frost that pricks the pine tree's swelling burrs,
The bind-weed and the sulphur flower,
The owl that brings the gilia's hour,
The blundering moth that to the primrose whirrs.
I trust I shall not miss the meadow grass
From fields elysian, nor the wind-rung bells
Of columbine among the asphodels.
Nor dipping willows where the waters pass,
I have no mind for harps and seraph's wings,
'Tis Heaven for me with all green growing things.

Editor's Notes

AU 329

[Make haste, the wild oats say]

Make haste, the wild oats say,
        The rain is falling,
Break ground, brook no delay,
        The Spring is calling.
Climbs up the rain wet steep
The herder and his sheep,
Let us make haste and grow, the wild oats say.

Editor's Notes

AU 333

March

In March the corn land stubble pales
Before the wind's bright flails;
And the blackbirds' whirling braid
Is scattered as seed to be summer's shade.

At the town's edge the human waste
Scurries in shame and haste,
Hopeful, as dust,
To the nearest rag-weed root to be laid;
And the tin-can heap augments its rust.

And what, with the stubble and dust are tossed,
For the cool March flaw to fling in my face—
Grit in my mouth of unreckoned cost,
And what was so sweet is a dusty taste—
Of the year's loves I have lost.

But when April comes with her kissing rain,
And sooth to the plough the warm earth yields,
I shall be out in the greening fields,
Planting young loves again.

Editor's Notes

AU 338; typescript and three carbon copies, one very clean.

The Naughty Jesus

Dust devils danced and swirled on the parched llano of San Juan.
Withered and yellow rustled the dying leaves of Indian corn.
For three days the Red Men danced the ceremonial rain dance,
Till the dust was ankle deep in the plaza and the corn maidens
fainted.
Still the Rain Gods sulked in the Jemez peaks beyond the
Rio Grande,
And maintained their hatred for the new Christian church gods.
Then appeared the desperate Indians before the padre of
the old mission.
"Lend us, Padre, the little Jesus to carry amidst our dying corn.
For pity he will bring us rain where our own gods have failed."
Soon afterwards came rushing great black clouds from the
west world.
Rain fell in swift torrents, bringing much hail and wind.
It beat the corn to the ground and left the fields in ruin.
The Indians took council and again appeared before the padre.
"Lend us now, oh Padre, Santa Maria, the mother of this
Christ child.
We would take her to our fields that she may herself see,
What her naughty little son Jesus has done to our fields of corn."

Editor's Notes

AU 371; single sheet with corrections. A drawing of a procession in New Mexico appears at the top of the sheet, with manuscript title.

Song

For me no more is splendor of the dawn,
Nor beauty in the fragrant star-lit hills;
The golden heart from out the day is gone,
No more is music in the summer rills.

The mighty wind that calleth from the deep
No more my soul to high emprise can win,
And thought unstirred must lowly levels keep—
Ah! where is now the glory that hath been?

What if we two but dreamed the earth was fair,
Or music aught but echoes from the heart—
If love be all the light of life, O where
Shall life find radiance if love depart?

Or shall I find it shining in thine eyes?
When through the fields of hyacinthine light,
My soul shall pass at last in sweet surprise
To find that life itself, not death, is night.

And we shall walk together hand in hand,
And hear again the voice of wind and stream,
And mid fair meadows in that lovely land,
Shall find again the glory and the dream.

Editor's Notes

AU 381; clean typescript also in *AU* 546.

AU 381 contains a notebook with Austin's note: "1899-1913; this book was used by me in Inyo, poems being copied in it as they were written. M. A." The handwritten copies in *AU* 381 are very clean.

Bartimeus

Tale hath not told if there be any lands
Where his strayed, stumbling feet and futile hands
Go not entreating, no, nor ever times,
Nor lordly cities reared in any climes
That him deny, nor princes, throned, elate,
That have not Bartimeus at the gate
To beg and wait.

Far known the shuffling step, and leperous palms,
And dolorous whine of him that asketh alms.
See where the white, night lamps for banquets flare
Rings through the hautboy's changes his despair,
And never saint goes purely up to pray
But findeth Bartimeus by the way,
Who "Jesus pity," doth insistent cry,
And "hark ye, Son of David, pass not by,
For blind am I."

The wandering stars go over him and call
Out of the deeps strong tides that trembling fall
Into the deep again with sharp, salt tears.
The spring has quickened through a thousand years
The sweet wild hyacinths on all the hills
Here of the purple blood the slain day spills,
And stark, high hills, and stubborn ranges grow
Divinely tender through the alpenglow,—
He doth not know.

He doth not see the reek of stinking lanes
Nor the low roof, scant purchase of his pains
Where his blind mate by deathbed cradle weeps
Nor the gaunt fates that stalk him while he sleeps.
Thronged with an eyeless crew, the lees of earth,

He mocks his death in life with joyless mirth
And "Peace," the people say, "he hath forgot,
What doth he lack or lose, he knoweth not
How vexed his lot."

And straight betwixt loud laughter and an oath
Breaks up the old world-pain, that stifles both,
To vex the dreamer whom the time befools
To think the strumpet learning of the schools
Could medicine the sight to those blank eyes,
Who shall upbraid when Bartimeus cries,
"Strong son of David, render me my sight,"
And hath Christ passed, and left no ray of light
To pierce his night?

Editor's Notes

AU 381

China

A long time coming all old ways, she turned
Deaf ear to strenuous strangers at her gate,
And then in idlewise, as if she spurned
The thought that such could vex her ancient state;
As if she scorned to say "Begone, depart,"
To jugglers mouthing in her thoroughfares,
Granted them leave of highway and of mart
A beggar's leave to cry their strumpet wares.

But when their clamor pierced her dreaming through,
The long thick dreaming of a thousand years,
Wits dulled by sleep the bolts of silence drew,
Beat down the guard that hedged her ancient fears,
Smote blind and large to give her slumbers ease—
Straight through her secret ways the tumult pours,
Alas! how shall she clear the house of these
Since she herself hath beaten down the doors!

Editor's Notes

AU 381

Providences

How can you think God would not take
Great care for all small things of everyday;
The sun across your garden hose can make
A rainbow of the spray.

Editor's Notes

AU 381

Syrinx

Now have I seen at dawn the red stag graze,
Now have I half forgot all human ways,
And wonder half that once I thought them good,
Now have I grown knee-deep into the wood.

Green glooms there are among the live oak trees
And small, wild, hairy things that lurk in these
Where all the wood is still, come forth and play.
And when there are two moons, one in the sky
And one dropped in the pool, I, tiptoe, spy
Young dryads dancing on the moon flecked sod
With nimble satyrs; and the Great Wood-god
Plucks up my stems and empties out the heart;
These notched and fashioned with a cutting stone,
And softly laid to lips and softly blown,
Speak all the thoughts in which the wood has part.

Blow, Wood-god, blow, until the happy reeds
Drip sounds as sweet as vagrant scent that leads
The moths o' moonless nights, to honeyed hollow;
Blow till its tender trill the wood-folk follow
And all the wind-wrung stalks will envy this,
So small a weed should know a wood-god's kiss.

Editor's Notes

AU 381; see *AU* 579, with punctuation as here.

Tears in the Night

Tears in the night, and sore unslaked desire,
Old wounds that ache, old dreams that throng and press,
Ignoble scorn, the cloak of weariness,
Slack hands that fail along the unstrung lyre;
Such pangs they have who labor and aspire
In that soul-sickness, dread of unsuccess,
And all their bread doth smack of bitterness
Besprent with ashes of Promethean fire.

Editor's Notes

AU 381

The Mill Wheel

So slow they are, the mills of God a-turning
To grind out the happier grist,—
How long the people will be, Lord, in earning
The wages they have missed!
They have given to Thy waters all their weeping
And their blood to overflow,
In the darkness they can hear the millrace sweeping
And the mill wheel turning slow.

On the threshing floor like patient muzzled cattle
They have trodden out the corn,
Where the earth is red with dewing of old battle
In keen days ere they were born.
"Not for ourselves," they say, "would we be minding
To drop down and die unfed,
But for our children, Lord, with all this grinding
Will you give them stones for bread?

"Not for ourselves but for the young, young races,
That come crowding at the birth,
We are stricken at the wheel to give them places
In the choked and acrid earth.
And we go down to the grave in mighty numbers,
Sick, before our time, to go,
But the grinding does not vex us in our slumbers,
And the mill wheel turneth slow."

How long, O Lord, the people will be learning
What is cast into their teeth,
That never wheel goes forward in its turning
If the dead drag underneath.
For they rise up from the choked and swollen sluices
Sodden things that clog and bind,

In the spume of outworn manners and old uses,
And the grist will never grind.

Goes not forward though the fecund earth has quickened
The young, white, strong-leaping springs,
For their mingling waters mantle, fouled and thickened
By all old unhappy things.
Mummied laws that have no Truth to thrill them,
And no power to waste or rot,
Husks of promises that have no Hope to fill them,
And the grist it grindeth not.

What faiths have they, and are not most beholden
To the ashen dead for them,
Their very God has thumbprints, left by moulding
Hands that struck the tents of Shem,
And they do His work on earth by funeral tapers,
Is no sun nor starshine overhead
In their firmament of baleful graveyard vapors,
And their saints are also dead.

How long with sick men's hearts will they be groping
The pale fields of Proserpine,
To sow salt barren acres, and be hoping
From withered grapes new wine.
Go hence and clear your rivers for God's torrents
Till his whirlwinds dredge their slime,
And the dead past let go seaward with the currents
Of a younger fuller time.

The young waters are the sweetest in their flowing,
The young sap makes fairest fruit,
The young blood has fullest pulse and ruddiest showing
The young tree takes quickest root;
And the young young races were it merely

For young scorn of such as we
Will grind out the finer grist and not be weary
Let them be, let them be.

The mills of God turn slowly, labored, droning
And the grist is hard to grind.
But they go not any faster for your groaning
You whom grave clothes chafe and bind.
Go not forward in the sweating and the weeping
For the rotting dead below,
They have stifled in the race, the waters sweeping,
And the mill wheel turneth slow.

Editor's Notes

AU 381

Brother-the-Wolf

Brother-the-wolf, 'tis the hour of the gloaming,
The gilias glow white and wild bees are homing,
The low wheeling sun through the rifts of the ranges
Yet lights the wild peaks in the long twilight changes.
The reek of the wood smoke hangs low on the hill,
The fold fires are lighted, the mesas all still,
The wind in the swale of the lupines flits free;
And the breath of the sage and the gilia flower
And the smell of the wood-smoke betoken the hour,
Brother-the-wolf, of your tryst with me.

Brother-the-wolf, now the elf owls are mating,
I lean from my rest in the cactus scrub waiting,
To hark their soft hooting and feather light whirring,
And hear the hare shriek where the red fox is stirring;
The sky like a burnished shield hollow and dim
Lit up by the balefires that glint on its rim
Grows keen in the east where the moon is to be,
And the little grey mice by the grass stalks that climb
To the moon of the mesas betokens the time,
Brother-the-wolf, that you run with me.

Brother-the-wolf, 'tis the night hours for waking
Till from Shoshone land dawn-end comes breaking,
Hot on the quarry trail answers your baying
Grey shape like your shape through the mellow dusk swaying;
Red eyes of the pack and the wind on the hill,
And warm, scented glooms that lie dreaming and still,
Wide wastes of the moonlight and shadows that flee,
And a breath on the cheek of that earlier time
When the man-seed was young and the earth in its prime,
Brother-the-wolf, as you run with me.

*

Brother-the-wolf, 'tis the end of our running,
Soon on the hill-slope the snake will be sunning,
Soon, soon from the mesa the shadows be failing
High in their airy haunts hawks will be sailing
Soon in their shallow forms rabbits will cower
And the sun shut the eyes of the moon gazing flower
Now the almond copse stirs to the blunt droning bee
And the breath of the dawn and the white morning glare
Bids the bat to his hole and thy breed to the lair,
Brother-the-wolf, and my work to me.

Editor's Notes

AU 381

[Once I heard my daffodils

Once I heard my daffodils,
Crowded in the slender glass,
Whisper; springeth now the grass
On the shouldering, seaward slopes
Where the purblind seafog gropes
Up the cañons of wet rills.

Still they said, the daffodils
Leaning from the crystal vase,
Now the wild oats grow apace
Where the strong sun warms the sod
By old trails the padres trod
On the poppy-breasted hills.

Gossiped thus the daffodils,
Now the blunt-faced bees carouse
Mid the high wind shaken boughs;
Quit O house-bound heart your pain
And by trails all sweet with rain
Find the young year in the hills!

Editor's Notes

AU 385: manuscript dated San Francisco, February 17, 1905.

[Oh my America!]

Oh my America,
        Not yet the motherland!

        Woman, sib to us, not too complaisant
        Whetting our powers with resistance not feigned
                but instinctive
        Yielding pleasure, woman wise, to the strong only;
        We, having proved our manhood upon you,
        Salute you!

        Not yet the motherland!

        And not even a grief to gnaw like an old bone
        Finds an old grief to gnaw on like a bone
        As well the river would complain that the shores
                go by too fast.

Editor's Notes

AU 418: untitled typescript
    sib = abbreviation of sibling

On Receiving a Book of Erotic Verse

Your verses sound, my friend,
Cradle and crash as a steep-shored surf,
        Or make long whispering runs on level beaches.

Your words are all sea colored,
        And under them your thoughts
        Waver like weed and tempt the diver's hand
        Taking the sea's tint, sapphire and amber pied,
        And semblance of its motion.

But all the hand brings back
Is slime and limpness.

Editor's Notes

AU 421: clean typescript.

Orchard Blossoms

Last night I brought orchard blossoms
Into the house; delicate, rose-lipt maiden
New budded apple boughs,
The pear trees white oblations,
Petal furred branches of plums
Wherein all day, till I cut them,
Bright banded bees made murmurous contentment.
Brought them into the house and set them
In yellow pitchers, black jars from San Ildefonso
And tall blue vases, to slake myself of their beauty,
Till the wild plum honey was grown
Faintly fetid of staleness, as petal by petal
Loveliness dropped unfruited,
Regaling his practiced sense with the summer steeped
Honey sweet scent of maiden fancy.

But why was I, later,
Vexed with my friend who gathered
Delicate, petal bright loves, regaling
His all too transient sense with the honey-sweet
Fragrance of maiden fancy;
Unless I had somehow felt
Guilty myself, on behalf of the orchard blossoms.

Editor's Notes

AU 430; clean typescript and two carbon copies
San Ildefonso is a Tewa pueblo near Santa Fe.

The Passing of the Flocks

I should like to be in Inyo
When the flocks go by again,
The long fleeced flocks and the wise old dogs,
And the long armed, bearded men.
When the tall, pale guidons of dust go by,
And the brush fires glow at night
Little and low on the mesa trail,
And the peaks are high and white.

All summer long in Inyo
There is nothing stirs on the trail
But the shy, scared young of the rabbit
And the scuttling broods of the quail.
But when you hear the coyote
At the end of the summer's heat
Howl for the grey of the dawning,
As he goes to seek his meat,

When the wind of the piñon harvest
Blows up the mouse grey mist,
And brown are the buds of the heather
Where they and the frost have kissed,
Then down come the flocks from the meadows
In the van of the forward snows,
And far at the foot of the mountain
The dust of their passing shows.

Then a herder will tell you a story
Of a mountain lion he slew,
And how he tracked it home to its lair,
Till he makes you wish it were you,
And one will tell of a bear in the night,
And one has an eaglet tame

Which he took from a dizzying eyrie
On a peak without a name.

Editor's Notes

AU 436; clean typescript

Inyo County is in the Owens Valley, on the eastern side of the Sierra Nevadas, including the towns of Lone Pine, Independence, and Bishop.

Penitente Ritual

While the Brothers whip themselves.

Now, altogether,
Come in on your knees
And praise the blood of this discipline.

Now on our knees,
We unite to implore
This blood of mine I am shedding.

I am a sinner
Who is now sworn
To praise the blood of this discipline.

Here in my loneness
There should accompany me
The whole universe in this discipline

With this destination
My Jesus came
To endure the blood of this discipline.

To this destination
Lord Jesus went
His body scored with stripes of this discipline.

His precious wounds,
Why did he have them?
In contemplation of this discipline.

In heavy sorrow
Lord Jesus went
In the persuasion of this discipline.

*

Heavy the beam
He bore on his shoulders
Heavy with sins of this discipline.

My God I implore
To grant me His grace
For the blood I have shed in this discipline.

To Holy Calvary
Come on your knees
Come and endure the blood of this discipline.

Editor's Notes

AU441; clean signed typescript.

For more on the ritual described here, see "The Trail of the Blood" in *Land of Journeys' Ending*, reprinted in *MASW*, 151–64.

The Procession of the Pines

I wish I knew what the pines are about
Marching over the hill,
From the wooded gap where the creek comes out
To hurry the saws of the mill,
Up and up where the cañon leads,
With hardly a gap or a stop,
The pines keep on in their stately way;
But never quite to the top.

The quaking aspens are stay-at-homes
And flutter their twinkling leaves
To the gossip of quiet neighborhoods
Which only the wind believes;
And round by the foothill coasts are set
The evergreen oaks, each one,
Like reverend grandsires of afternoons,
Taking their ease in the sun;
The willows follow the white-foot streams
And grow at the water's will;
But ever and always the pines keep on
Marching over the hill.
Darkly they troop by butte and pass,
Riving great rocks for place,
And the foremost ones are bent and bowed
Like runners stretched in a race.

But if I look from the highest peaks,
Which never the pines attain,
There they go down on the other side
And over the hill again.
Down where the high walled cañon leads,
Into the valleys and out,
Still the procession of pines keeps on;

But what is it all about?

Editor's Notes

AU 465; manuscript noted "Independence Cal."; two more drafts and a carbon copy.

Sea Gardens

Come to the deep sea gardens
Where the fringed anemones grow,
With moss grown shells,
And white foam-bells,
And limpets all in a row.

Down in the deep sea gardens
At the lowest ebb of the tide,
The sea snails feed
In the slippery weed,
And purple urchins hide.

There in the deep sea gardens
Where the painted starfish creep,
Where pink shrimps play
In the rockweed gay,
The wee crabs scuttle and peep.

Come to the deep sea gardens
Where the barnacles cluster white,
Where mussels cling,
Till the long tides swing
And cover them out of sight.

Editor's Notes

AU 515; clean typescript.

A Sea-Side Episode

The hermit crab, the horse-shoe crab,
The hard-shelled crab, these three,
They ran a race
On a sandy place
On a splashy beach by the sea.

A fat sea-urchin marked the goal,
As they all stood up in a row
With intent to prove
Who could fastest move,
When the star-fish shouted, Go!

They lifted up their six queer legs
And all struck out with a will,
And the race was done,
But every one
Had the same opinion still.

Editor's Notes

AU 518; clean typescript.

The Shameful Dream

There are four tapers at my side,
The wicks wink dull and red,
Four saints upon the walls abide.
The cross hangs by my bed;
And though my pillow is not wide
It holds another head.

Four crosses turn upon the vane
That whines above the roof,
All hours the wagging winds complain
To put them to the proof.
But neither cross nor saints restrain
Nor keep my dream aloof.

It does not come by day,
Nor yet by candle light,
Nor when the woods are grey
And skies are morning bright,
But when no stars array
The shut, dead hours of night.

I know the face it wears
My days would shun to meet;
I know what name it bears,
What shames must dog its feet;
But through my sleep it fares
Most dear, and aching sweet.

When dark doth like a mist
The dank, wild fens out-creep,
It hales me to the tryst
I am right glad to keep,

When I my dream have kissed
In deep, blind lanes of sleep.

I am come to the prime of years
And have both praise and fee,
Upon my face no scar of tears
Is there for men to see,
And no man else but God who rears
The hand of scorn at me.

But between my dream and morn
Before the night murk breaks,
When the day star is not born
And yet no bird awakes,
Before that hand of scorn
My spirit sits and quakes.

It is not for the evil blow
But the blow that I let be,
And the work my hand let go
When the sword was out and free,
For the strength my arm should owe
My dream has stol'n from me.

I am two score years and ten
And am both peer and knight,
But I dare not think of the moment when
Great Christ shall make it light,
And with me stand before all men
The dream I dreamed at night.

Editor's Notes

AU 523; clean manuscript, dated 1896.

[Small were they Twain]

Small were they Twain,
        Small and misshapen;
Strong were they Twain,
        Strong and hard favored;
Enduringly thoughtful were they Twain,
        Enduring of will;
Unyieldingly thoughtful were they Twain,
        Unyielding of will:

Swiftly thoughtful were they Twain,
        Swift of wile;
Heartless minded were they Twain,
        Wrathful of heart;
Strong were they of spirit,
        Strong were they of breath,
Evil were they and bad,
        Evil, both, and bad.

Editor's Notes

AU 538; clean typescript.

A Song for the Good Moment

Open your heart to laughter
Ere the good moment slips
Past the grave guard of the eyes
To the keen, curved thirst of the lips.

Now while my blood sings to you
While the pulse streams quick with fire
And banner-wise the spirit strains
In the wind of high desire

While in the outer reaches
The live thoughts meet and close
Laugh—so we shall not whimper
When the good moment goes.

What is this that stirs beside me
What sweet troubling
In the darkness, in the farthest reaches,
It is the thought that quickens to my friend.

Lay your thought to mine, O my friend,
In the silence, in the secret places,
They shall beget great deeds between them.

Editor's Notes

AU 547; manuscript.

Compare the Chisera's song in *The Arrow Maker* and "Song of the Mateless Woman" in *The American Rhythm* (1923).

The Swallows

Farewell, and take thy flight
And take thy flight
Across the blue,
But Oh, forget not
One who weeps,
Who weeps for you.

Forget thou never there are eyes
That only know to weep for you,
And in thy griefs and thy delights
Forever at thy side,
Forever at thy side
Seeks only you.

Editor's Notes

AU 577; typescript with heading "Canciones del Rio Grande."

To Mary Vallette

If stars have power,
Then I commend you
To that white orb that rules the twilight
Like a contented wife beside the moon.

If stars have power
Then she should bring you
The recollected hour by saints invited
Between the night's complexities and naked noon.
None but homecoming sounds should greet you,
White radiance and a rosy stain,
The day a glory and the dusk a croon,—
If stars have power.

Editor's Notes

AU 595; clean typescript and one carbon copy.

[To the right—the mountains wide eyed—]

To the right—the mountains wide eyed—
Stretching out of their wisping circlet of snow—
To the left the road spins past in a stone tracked trail
Clasping an adobe house
With a pen for its cow.
A few penitent cedars
Dwarfed, but firmly ensconced,
And prattling in and about,
Tunefully grazing,
Goats pass, or pause, abashed.
Below, the acequia winds its blue threaded way—
The air, all sifted clear—
Seems pressed, in a crystal cup,
While heaven shines through it, in sparkling darts.
Suddenly swinging through space
Is a silvery cloud—
Up, up it flutters above my head,
And I hold my breath for the downward curve.
Up again starry flight—in your circling sea—
You are bearing to me,
Aglow, 'neath your silvery wing—
The spun blue of heaven you've circled within.
You swoop round and about, delving,
Then swoop down anew—
Tell, can you tell which is the true—
If you're me—
Or—I'm you?

Editor's Notes

AU 596; manuscript and typescript.

The Unbeliever

I heard one crying in the market place,
"The Gods, the Gods are dead!"
Wan he was and sere,
A rain blanched forest leaf,
And his cry was clear
As the grasshopper's high note
Shrilled by failing pastures drear;
And with his wailing smote
A chill through all the summer atmosphere.

Slacked all the feet of trade
To give his wailing ear,
The idlers loitering in the shade
Began to flout and jeer;
And one across the wine jar's rim,
Made keen by drink, called after him,
"The Gods, they have been dead this twenty year."

And one to make the merrier jest his own,
Had mocked his shambling step and piping tone,
"The Gods are not yet dead, my friend, for why?
In truth the Gods must live before they die."

But still he wailed, and with his wailing woke
The temple echoes, while the vestal train
Poured with their incense pitying disdain;
And high above the sacrificial smoke
Hot breath of cursing broke
From priests whose white wrath leaped like altar flame,
And all the humble folk
Who with devoted garlands came,
Cast stones and spat, and the Gods did call,
As for such sacrilege a bolt must fall.

*

So from the ways of them the wailer passed
Mocked, cursed, and stoned, until his last
Scant shadow crossed their dim horizon line,
Only the Most High Gods had made no sign!

Editor's Notes

AU 615; see *AU* 381; typescript with corrections.

Whose Children?

How will it fare with the peace we have made for our children,
With the order and seemliness,
In the days when our children
Divide the rule of the earth with men made wolfish by hunger,
Showing its fangs long after
In sudden, unreckoning rancors.
How will it be when the light we have won for our children
Is darkened by brains befumbled
For the lack of the crumbs that fall from our childrens' tables;
When the men that our children
Must trade with, work with—or fight with
Remember the years of their hunger,
How will it be in that day
With our children?

Editor's Notes

AU 639; typescript with a note at the end, "Written for the Russian Children's Famine Relief, Feb. 14, 1922."

Wisdom

Three Kings they came to Bethlehem,
They were both good and wise,
But they did not know where Heaven lay
Till it was blazoned from the skies.

The Shepherd folk of Bethlehem
For their Redeemer prayed,
But they must have a seraph choir
To show where he was laid.

The oxen and the asses stood
In Bethlehem's lowly stall,
They did not see the wandering star,
Nor hear the angels call,
But with the asses' mind they knew,
With heart of kine they felt,
And by their Lord in manger laid
Without a sign *they* knelt.

Editor's Notes

AU 646; typescript and carbon copy, both clean.

[By the Deer's Cry]

You should have loved me by the Deer's Cry,
There at Jemez.

Snow crisp as ash on the fire-red mountain bosses,
Gilt of the falling waters,
Dawn blue, out of the soft blackness
Of midnight paling
To the flail of the kiva drums,
All night, till our hearts are beaten
One with the earth-heart.

You should have loved me by the Deer's Cry,
There at Jemez.

Dawn blue beaten out of thick blackness
By the flail of the kiva drums,
And come, come, come, say the *tombes*,
There where the medicine women
Call by the earth-power, power of women,
And the great males of the deer kind
Come down from the mountain.

Editor's Notes

AU 654; three typescripts in various stages.

Deer's Cry is a ceremonial dance to bring bucks down from the mountain. Jemez names the river and the pueblo.

When I Am Dead

This is what I shall do
When I am dead.

When the hot wind frets not
Nor the sharp sleet;
When weariness wears not my heart,
Nor stones my feet;
When the fire's spell is unbound
And I faint no more for bread;—
How well I know what I shall do
When I am dead!

I shall take a white road
On a warm last-lighted hill,
Where saffron-shod the evening goes,
Where the pale gilias unclose
And the flitter-moths are still.

I shall take a high road where the flock scent lingers
In the browsed sage and the blue, bush-lupine fingers,
I shall find a by-road by the foot changes
Till I come where the herders' fires
Blossom in the dusk of the grape-colored ranges.

And I shall sit by the bedding fires
With the little, long-armed men,
Eleheverray and Little Pete and Narcisse Julienne—
They being even as I, and all of us being dead—
For what can come when sense decays
And the dull flesh fails,
But that man is one with his thought at last

And the Wish prevails?

*

So it shall be day an we will,
With a burnished blue hot sky,
And a heat dance over the open range
Where tall pale guidons of dust go by.
Or it shall be dark, as we choose,
At the lambing pens under Temblor hill
With the mothering mutter of the ewes
And a wind to which the herd grass cowers,
While the dogs edge in to the watching fires
And darkly the procreant earth suspires.

So it shall be when Balzar the Basque
And the three Manxmen
And Pete Giraud and my happy ghost
Walk with the flocks again.

Editor's Notes

AU 629; early typescript and subsequent drafts; the carbon copy incorporates all corrections.

Published posthumously, with a eulogy by T. M. Pearce, in *New Mexico Quarterly* 4 (August 1934): 233–35; printed privately by the Rydal Press, Santa Fe, New Mexico, by permission of the executors of the Estate of Mary Austin, 1935. Both printed texts have the fifth stanza as follows, but the typescripts and syntax suggest the printing I have given:

And I shall sit by the bedding fires
With the little, long-armed men,
Eleheverray and Little Pete and Narcisse Julienne—
For what can come when sense decays
They being even as I, and all of us being dead—
And the dull flesh fails,
But that man is one with his thought at last
And the Wish prevails?

Selected Bibliography ✱ *Indexes*

Selected Bibliography

Works by Mary Austin

The Land of Little Rain. Boston: Houghton Mifflin, 1903.

The Flock. Boston: Houghton Mifflin, 1906. Reprinted by the University of Nevada Press, 2001.

The Arrow-Maker: A Drama in Three Acts. Revised edition. Boston: Houghton Mifflin, 1915.

The Land of Journeys' Ending. New York: Century, 1924. Reprinted by the University of Illinois Press, 2003.

Stories from the Lost Borders. Edited by Marjorie Pryse. New Brunswick, NJ: Rutgers University Press, 1987.

Cactus Thorn. Reno: University of Nevada Press, 1988.

Beyond Borders: Selected Essays of Mary Austin. Edited by Reuben J. Ellis. Carbondale: Southern Illinois University Press, 1996.

Mary Austin's Southwest: An Anthology of Her Literary Criticism. Edited by Chelsea Blackbird and Barney Nelson. Salt Lake City: University of Utah Press, 2005.

Works about Mary Austin

Goodman, Susan, and Carl Dawson. *Mary Austin and the American West*. Berkeley: University of California Press, 2008.

Pearce, T. M. *Literary America, 1903–1934: The Mary Austin Letters*. Westport, CT: Greenwood Press, 1979.

Schaefer, Heike. *Mary Austin's Regionalism: Gender, Genre, and Geography*. Charlottesville: University of Virginia Press, 2004.

Stineman, Esther Lanigan. *Mary Austin: Song of a Maverick*. New Haven, CT: Yale University Press, 1989.

Index of Titles

Index of First Lines

JAMES PERRIN WARREN is S. Blount Mason Jr. Professor of English at Washington and Lee University. His scholarship and teaching over the past thirty years have focused on nineteenth-century American literature and environmental literature. He has recently completed *Other Country*, a book about Barry Lopez and the community of artists, and he is beginning a new project on the poetry and prose of John Haines.